James Dobson's

GOSPEL

of

Self-Esteem

& Psychology

Martin & Deidre Bobgan
EastGate Publishers

Scripture quotations, unless noted otherwise, are from the Authorized King James Verison of the Bible.

James Dobson's Gospel of Self-Esteem & Psychology

Revised edition of **Prophets of PsychoHeresy II**

Copyright © 1990, 1998 Martin and Deidre Bobgan
Published by EastGate Publishers
Santa Barbara, California

Library of Congress Catalog Card Number 98- 93727
ISBN 0-941717-16-X

Printed in the United States of America

This book is dedicated to those Christians who place their confidence in the cross of Christ, the Word of God and the work of the Holy Spirit, rather than in the psychological opinions of men.

We are grateful to Dr. Jay Adams for his reading and critiquing the original manuscript. He has been a great help to us in our writing. We also wish to thank Jim and Ronnie Gail Bowlan, Rick and Gail Miesel, and Gary and Carol Milne. Each couple helped with the original volume. They have also been an encouragement to us.

For a sample copy of a free newsletter about the intrusion of psychological counseling theories and therapies into Christianity, please write to:

PsychoHeresy Awareness Ministries
4137 Primavera Road
Santa Barbara, CA 93110

or

phone: 1-800-216-4696

e-mail: bobgan@psychoheresy-aware.org

Web Site Address:

www.psychoheresy-aware.org

Table of Contents

1

Reasons for Concern

Criticisms of James Dobson's work are hard to find, largely because popular Christian writers and broadcasters, despite their influence, are rarely accorded a thoughtful critique.

Christianity Today[1]

Over thirty years ago we began comparing and contrasting psychotherapy and its underlying psychologies with what the Bible teaches. In addition to looking at the various counseling theories and methodologies, we examined research having to do with that kind of psychology. During that time we read all or parts of thousands of research studies and hundreds of books on the subject.

Nearly twenty years ago we completed our first book, *The Psychological Way / The Spiritual Way,* which we had hoped would stem the rising tide of psychology in the church. However, since then psychology has strengthened its grip and widened its span throughout Christendom. In our book *PsychoHeresy* we began naming names of leaders in the movement who amalgamate psychology and Scripture. Following that we wrote *Prophets of PsychoHeresy I*, in which we specifically and more extensively critiqued the works of Dr. Gary Collins, Dr. Lawrence Crabb, Jr., Dr. Paul Meier, and Dr. Frank Minirth.

In this present volume we critique Dr. James C. Dobson, who is influential in promoting the psychologizing of Christianity. The original title was *Prophets of PsychoHeresy II*. However, we have changed the title and reduced the length of this revised version. Just as in *Prophets of PsychoHeresy I*, we used the word *prophet* to mean a spokesman for a cause or movement. The heresy involved is the departure from absolute confidence in the Word of God for all matters of life and conduct and a movement towards faith in the unproven, unscientific psychological opinions of men. Thus we call it "psychoheresy."

As in our other books, when we speak of psychology we are **not** referring to the entire discipline. Our concern is with that part of psychology which deals with the very nature of man, how he should live, and how he should change. That includes the theories and methodologies behind psychological counseling, clinical counseling, psychotherapy, and the psychological aspects of psychiatry. The same theories have also influenced certain aspects of educational psychology, especially the theories of behaviorism and humanism. Because these theories deal with the nonphysical aspects of the person, they intrude upon the very essence of biblical doctrines of man, including his fallen condition, salvation, sanctification, and relationship of love and obedience to God.

We have changed the title in this updated version to *James Dobson's Gospel of Self-Esteem and Psychology* to indicate the contents more precisely. We contend that self-esteem teachings compromise the preaching and hearing of the true Gospel. Psychotherapy and its underlying psychologies undermine the clear Gospel with the wisdom of men about which Paul warned in 1 Corinthians 1 and 2. When these theories and methodologies are added to the Word of God, one ends up with a counterfeit means of sanctification.

Because of his tremendous influence in bringing psychology and self-esteem teachings into the church, Dr. James Dobson's work is an appropriate subject for examination. Therefore what he has written and said will be examined from both a biblical and scientific point of view.

We are aware that there are pluses to Dobson's ministry. However, after all the pluses and minuses are added together, we conclude that Focus on the Family is an organization that too often honors man and his opinions over God and His Word. While there are times when Dobson presents biblical ideas in a sound manner, too much of what he espouses and teaches is based on unproven notions from secular psychology. Then, because he does teach some orthodox biblical concepts, such as the need for salvation and the value of prayer, his listeners may easily conclude that when he teaches psychological concepts he is not departing from a firm biblical foundation. In fact, Dobson assures his readers that his teachings *"originated* with the inspired biblical writers who gave us the foundation for all relationships in the home."[2] (Emphasis his.)

Contrary to what he claims, we will demonstrate that some of Dobson's basic assumptions and many of his specific teachings actually originated from secular psychological theorists whose opinions are based on godless foundations. Thus, Dobson uses the Bible as a sanction for dispensing unbiblical ideas to unsuspecting readers and listeners. The use of psychology to help people eclipses the Scriptures at Focus on the Family. Self-esteem and psychology are the two major thrusts that too often supersede sin, salvation, and sanctification. They are another gospel.

While identifying the names of individuals and ministries, we have been aware of the sensitivities of those we critique and their followers. We continue to offer to meet publicly with any of the individuals we have critiqued to discuss what they and we have said. The editor of *Christian News* attempted to get a response from Dobson by printing parts of *Prophets of PsychoHeresy II* along with an open letter to Dobson. Dobson did respond, but he did not respond to the issues at hand. Instead he made ad hominem remarks about what he supposed our motives might be, including greed, supposing that we were trying to make money by criticizing him. However, during our years of writing, we have understood that if we wanted to write a best seller we should write in the same vein as those we criticize. A desire for popularity and profit would take us in a different direction from the way we are going. While all of our books are well researched, none is popular. Nevertheless, certain issues must be addressed and certain teachings must be examined, especially when these are being promulgated by popular, powerful figures.

There seems to be an all pervasive misology, which is unbiblical and contrary to what the history of the church reveals. This misology exists not only among those we criticize, but also among their followers. For the most unbiblical reasons they condemn anyone who dares criticize popularizers of psycho-scriptural amalgamation. Unfortunately those men have achieved a new status in the church, a type of Protestant popery with its attributed infallibility.

It is imperative that the church look again at the example of the Bereans in the book of Acts. They "searched the Scriptures daily, whether these things were so." What things? The things that Paul and Silas told them. Too many Christians fail to search the Scriptures to see whether or not the pronouncements of popular preachers and teachers are true. Even those who search the Scriptures concerning other matters refuse to examine the teachings of those who promote psychotherapy and its underlying psychologies and mix them with Scripture.

It seems cataclysmically contradictory to see professors at Bible colleges and seminaries, who are supposed to be specialists in the Old and New Testaments and who carry such titles as Professor of Theology, stand idly by in this unbiblical rising tide of psychology which has engulfed the Bible colleges, seminaries and churches. Their silence proclaims their naiveté or ignorance and contradicts their degrees and titles. By their silence, such faculty members are doubly responsible for the rise of psychology in the church. Those who have been trained in the Word who do not act as wisely as the Bereans are doubly culpable. Their silence is a loud testimony to their reluctance to stop the psychologizing even though such psychologizing inevitably degrades God's Word.

Dr. J. Vernon McGee expressed concern over the psychologizing of Christianity, which he contended "will absolutely destroy Bible teaching and Bible churches."[3] In an article titled "Psycho-Religion—The New Pied Piper" he wrote:

> If the present trend continues, Bible teaching will be totally eliminated from Christian radio stations as well as from TV and the pulpit. This is not a wild statement made in an emotional moment of concern. Bible teaching is being moved to the back burner of broadcasting, while so-called Christian psychology is put up front as Bible solutions to life's problems.

In the same article he declared, "So-called Christian psychology is secular psychology clothed in pious platitudes and religious rhetoric."[4]

All of the research presented in the original volume has been even more conclusively supported by further research, right up to the present. The research documentation clearly demonstrates that Dobson is dreadfully wrong about both self-esteem and psychology. John Leo's *U.S News & World Report* article (1998) titled "Damn, I'm Good" followed his examination of the research on self-esteem. Leo says:

> The self-esteem movement is one of the marvels of our time. It goes on and on, even though its assumptions are wrong and its basic premises have been discredited by a great deal of research. Like a monster in the last 10 minutes of a horror movie, it has enough fatal wounds to stop a platoon. But it keeps stumbling on, seeming not to notice.[5]

Based on hundreds of research studies, Dr. Robyn Dawes, professor at Carnegie-Mellon University and a widely recognized researcher on psychological evaluations, declares:

... there is no positive evidence supporting the efficacy of professional psychology. There are anecdotes, there is plausibility, there are common beliefs, yes—but there is no good evidence.[6]

Because of all the research on psychotherapy and for numerous other reasons related to the practice of psychotherapy, such as the use of mental health professionals as experts in court and other realms of life, people are becoming concerned. Many are also concerned about the false teachings of self-esteem. There is now a plethora of theological and academic evidence to support the contents of this present volume and to severely contradict Dobson's position. Dobson's gospel of self-esteem and psychology is not the Gospel of Jesus Christ; it is neither theologically nor academically supported.

As we have continually stated in the past, we are not discussing the faith of any of the individuals we critique. Instead we are evaluating their teachings. As with previous people we have critiqued, we are hereby offering to meet publicly with Dobson. His tremendous popularity and influence increase his responsibility to make sure that he is biblically and scientifically sound in all that he is doing. We think he is not and invite him to show us that we are wrong.

2

Psychological Savior

Dr. James C. Dobson is one of the most influential spokespersons in the evangelical spectrum of Christianity. Millions of Christians have listened to his daily "Focus on the Family" broadcast and over fifty million people have viewed his "Focus on the Family" film series. Dobson's books are not only best sellers, but remain on the best-seller lists for years. His *Focus on the Family* magazine and church bulletin inserts supply weekly and monthly fare along with his books. His Focus on the Family ministry continues to expand its borders. According to *U.S. News & World Report* (1998):

> [Dobson's] radio and TV broadcasts are heard or seen by 28 million people a week. A core audience of 4 million listens to his *Focus on the Family* radio show every day. That gives him a greater reach than either Jerry Falwell or Pat Robertson at the height of their appeal. Dobson's most popular books have sold more than 16 million copies, and his other tracts and pamphlets have sold millions more.[1]

Dobson may indeed be the best-known and most respected man in twentieth-century American Christendom. An astounding number of Christians look to Dobson as an authority. His opinions and advice about children, the family, marriage, and society are held in high esteem. In fact, they are hardly considered opinions. They are received as authoritative truth. That's because of the current faith in psychology, especially when it is psychology practiced by a professing Christian.

While in past centuries such a revered position of authority among Christians would no doubt have been held by a theologian or pastor, Dobson came into his position through secular education. He holds the now-coveted title of "psychologist" rather than "theologian," although he was actually trained in education. He earned a Ph.D. in Education with a major in Child Development from the University of Southern California. According to the State of California Psychology Examining Committee, Dobson holds a generic license. A letter from that State office says:

> The license provided for in California law is a *generic* license. Given, however, the wide variety of activities in which psychologists engage, the Examining Committee allows candidates to specify an area of emphasis for oral examination. Dr. Dobson indicated "educational psychology" as his area of competency when he completed his oral examination in 1968. . . . Under the generic license requirements one is titled "licensed psychologist" in California.[2]

Dobson has made the most of that title. Countless Christians look to Dobson as an authority on all matters of life and conduct because he carries both titles: "psychologist" and "Christian," which is the new ideal in the contemporary church. The opening words of an article in *Christianity Today* refer to him as one "who may well be the most famous psychologist in the world."[3] However, *Christianity Today* also admits:

Dobson is a generalist and a popularist. That is an American tradition: speaking with authority and without footnotes. . . . If Dobson were more qualified in his assertions, if he developed careful biblical and theological arguments, if he marshaled psychological data for his positions, it is doubtful that he would sell millions of books.[4]

Dobson's teachings are psychological in theory and practice. His discussions about the nature of children and adults and how to change behavior come primarily from psychology rather than from the Bible. In numerous instances, they come from that kind of psychology which is opinion and not science. While Dobson opposes the teachings of some psychologists, he embraces the theories and practices of others. Like most practitioners, he is eclectic in his approach in that he picks and chooses from a variety of theorists. However, his psychology is neither original nor biblically based.

Dobson has not developed a new system of understanding and treating people. Nor do his psychological pronouncements and recommendations originate from a careful exegesis of Scripture, even though he sometimes uses the Bible to bolster up his psychological teaching. Dobson uses the story-telling mode, which not only keeps his readers' interested but gives a seeming reality to everything he says, including the ideology behind the details he chooses and the conclusions he makes.

Rather than relying on research, which may actually prove just the opposite from some of his conclusions, Dobson uses case histories which emphasize and especially dramatize the points he wants to make. But these considerations do not seem to bother the many Christians who base daily decisions on what Dobson says. In fact, his psychological influence on how to understand the nature of children and adults extends beyond denominational boundaries. By avoiding certain theological doctrines and questions, Dobson has made himself welcome in a great variety of religious settings.

Man of the Hour

Dobson's rise to fame tells us as much about the condition of Christianity as about the man himself. He chose to promote psychology at the right time as far as the church was concerned. The encroachment of the psychological way into Christianity has been a subtle gradual movement which began in seminaries and pastoral counseling classes. Pastors were concerned about their parishioners seeking help outside the fold and so they availed themselves of the wisdom of men in order to minister to souls.[5] While they may not have intentionally borrowed ideas and techniques which obviously contradict Scripture, they embraced enough to let the proverbial camel's nose into the tent.

Liberal denominations became psychologized much earlier than the more conservative ones, but there were a number of psychologists who were active in breaking down barriers of mistrust. Society as a whole was becoming saturated with the kind of psychology that seeks to understand why people are the way they are and how they change. Psychological language had become a part of everyday language and psychological solutions were being accepted as life's solutions. Sometimes, through the work of local mental health organizations, psychologists and ministers dialogued together, and in the process pastors became intimidated and psychologists received referrals.

Pastors accepted the lie that they could only deal with spiritual matters (with a very limited definition) and that only those who were psychologically trained were equipped to deal with psychological matters (which virtually included everything about understanding the nature of man and how to help him change). A number of evangelical Christians became psychologists and set about to educate the church regarding the importance of psychological theories and therapies in the lives of Christians. One of those men, Dr. Clyde Narramore, was instrumental in encouraging Dobson to pursue his interest in psychology.[6]

In addition to the active role of psychologists working to infiltrate the church, the passive role of worldly influence also seduced the church into a psychological mind-set. As Martin Gross says, we live in *The Psychological Society.*[7] Psychological opinions and explanations are everywhere, so much so that they are accepted as fact. And whenever a person is experiencing problems, the primary recommendation is, "You need to talk to a counselor"—that is, a professional, psychologically-trained counselor.

Most fundamental, evangelical Christians were suspicious of those psychological ideas which directly and obviously contradicted what they understood to be biblical. Therefore, they desired a form of psychology which seemed to agree with what they knew about the Bible. They were eager for a person who was both a psychologist and a Christian, a person who seemed to oppose secularism, but at the same time would deliver the supposed riches gleaned from the psychological mines. The church was ripe to embrace a psychological savior. Thus Dobson's psychological teachings and his mode of presentation captured the hearts of many.

His first book, *Dare to Discipline*,[8] was a breath of fresh air to Christian parents who were lost in the fog of permissiveness as promoted by secular psychologists and educators. Dobson rightly criticized the proponents of permissiveness and their humanistic philosophy, which allowed a child to do almost whatever he wanted, with the idea that eventually he would respond positively to the parents' tolerance, patience, and permissiveness.

Christians who were familiar with child-rearing admonitions in Scripture were uncomfortable with the teachings of permissiveness. They were relieved to find a readable book by a Christian educator and "psychologist" who seemed to teach biblical methods of child rearing. Here was a licensed psychologist confirming what conservative Christian parents believed to be right. But, Dobson was not just some "lowly" pastor teaching about raising children from a biblical perspective. He was a psychologist who could give authoritative, pragmatic, psychological reasons and methods for disciplining children. He was a "psychologist" who could stand up to those other psychologists who had been preaching the permissive way.

Dobson quickly endeared himself to mothers and fathers all over the nation. *Dare To Discipline* gave Christian parents the courage to discipline with spanking, at about the same time secular psychologists and educators were noting the negative effects of permissiveness. Christians knew that the Bible included spanking as one disciplinary means, but they had been intimidated by the opinions of psychological "experts." Therefore it was good news to have a Christian who was also a psychologist tell them that it is not only okay to spank, but necessary and effective. Dobson gave them a psychological rationale for a biblical method of child training. *Dare To Discipline* was an immediate best seller that established Dobson as an authority on child rearing.

The overwhelming response to Dobson's first book illustrates three things. First, Christians were being intimidated by secular educators and secular psychologists. Second, they would not have been intimidated if they had not already developed a high regard for psychology. Third, their high regard for psychology was no doubt based upon the mistaken assumption that psychological theories and therapies are scientific and therefore true. In fact, these three statements explain the solid faith that Christians have in psychology, especially when the psychology is preached and practiced by Christians. Somehow, they think that wedding psychology with Christianity produces the best truth of all.

Motherhood and Apple Pie

Dobson has a strong emotional appeal to women. He encourages mothers who elect to stay home with their young children instead of being pressured to have another career. He takes a strong stand on the importance of the parent-child relationship. In a superb folksy, down-home manner, undergirded with the titles "Dr." and "psychologist," Dobson gives assurance and counsel to wives and mothers. He especially endears himself to women with remarks such as:

> To the exhausted and harassed new mother, let me say, "Hang tough! You are doing *the* most important job in the universe!"[9] (Emphasis his.)

> I am especially sympathetic with the mother who is raising a toddler or two and an infant at the same time. There is no more difficult assignment on the face of the earth.[10]

Here is a man who appears to understand the trials and tribulations of womanhood. And, here is a man who even attempted to assist women by writing *What Wives Wish their Husbands Knew about Women*. Dobson's books ooze with examples of his own love and commitment to his wife and children. Thus he appears to be the perfect specimen of husband and father. And his daily radio program makes him available to women all over the country who are married to men who probably do not measure up to the Dobson image.

Along with all of his support, Dobson also engenders just enough fear to make women insecure about rearing children without his psychological understanding and teaching. One of his methods is through telling horror stories. For example, he stresses the importance of disciplining a so-called strong-willed child by telling the story about a girl who lost her eyesight by looking at the sun, even though she had been told not to, and suggests that the parents read the story to their children in hopes of preventing a similar tragedy.[11] He dramatizes a story of Lee Harvey Oswald's life to illustrate his point that inferiority and low self-esteem lead to disaster.[12] His stories of extreme situations of parental failure and childhood disaster capture attention. They also create fear that if parents don't do everything right, their children may have similar catastrophes.

While he gives great emotional encouragement to mothers, Dobson also appears to hold them responsible for their children's failures. He tells a story about himself when he caused pain to a new boy in his Sunday school class by calling his ears "Jeep Fenders." He claims he had no idea that he was embarrassing the boy with his joke. Therefore, he does not hold himself responsible for his insensitivity. Instead, he says:

> Looking back on the episode, I hold my teachers and my parents responsible for that event. They should have told me what it feels like to be laughed at . . . especially for something different about your body.[13]

Thus it was not his fault for making fun of another child. It was his parents' fault and it was his teacher's fault. It is hard to imagine that they had both neglected to teach him the rudimentary principles of thoughtfulness.

While the fear of the Lord is the beginning of wisdom, Dobson engenders a different kind of fear in parents. Parents who are conscientious about raising their children and who read Dobson's expansive repertoire of case histories may very well become fearful that no matter what they do they may harm junior's self-esteem. After listing ways a child's self-esteem can be damaged, Dobson says:

> . . . whereas a child can lose self-esteem in a thousand ways, the careful reconstruction of his personal worth is usually a slow, difficult process.[14]

Even his choice of words, such as "irreparable damage," "there is no escape,"[15] and the "damaged" child[16] can engender fear in the heart of every caring parent. With such engendered fear, a parent may feel an ominous sense of guilt regarding the possibility of failing to build the child's self-esteem. But, according to Dobson, guilt is dangerous too. He says:

. . . through some mystery of perception, a child can usually "feel" hidden guilt in his parents. . . guilt can be another formidable barrier in building self-respect among the young.[17]

Then rather than directing his reader to the Lord and His Word concerning whether he is truly guilty according to God's standards, confessing actual guilt, receiving forgiveness, and repenting, Dobson would have him consider what William Glasser says about the value of guilt.[18] Glasser stresses the importance of right and wrong, but refuses to accept the Bible as the standard for right and wrong. Why must the Christian parent turn to Glasser rather than the Lord?

Not even loving the child guarantees the kind of self-esteem that Dobson believes is so very necessary, for he says:

However, I have observed that many children know intuitively that they are loved by their parents, but they do not believe they are held in high esteem by them.[19]

What's a parent to do? Read Dobson. That's what. Or, listen to him on the radio. Without his strategies for helping the child develop self-esteem, the child may be doomed to a life of inferiority, self-doubt, low self-esteem, and failure.

Pragmatism

Dobson has given a fair amount of helpful recommendations to parents, such as the usefulness of consistency in discipline, guidelines for defining and enforcing boundaries for obedience, and other practical ways that discipline can be implemented. But, the consistent underlying rationale for his theories and methods of discipline is that they work. At least he believes and teaches that they work. One will find a heavy emphasis on pragmatism throughout Dobson's writings.

One cannot fully fault Dobson for his reliance on pragmatism because of the influence of psychology in the church. We are living in an era in which sole biblical authority has been looked down upon. Psychologists have led the way in deprecating obedience to any external set of rules or standards, unless, of course, they are psychological. In their attempt to free people from moral restraints of religion, psychology discourages *should's*, *ought's* and *must's* and replaces admonitions to obey God with psychological notions about what works. Because of this psychological influence, Christians often require a reason for obedience beyond the stated will of God. Even when God's Word is clear on an issue, there must be the added pragmatic reason for obedience. Thus faith in whether a plan of action will work may subtly or not so subtly supersede faith in God's Word.

Psychology

Dobson is to be commended for his strong teachings on combining firm discipline with love and affection in contrast to those child psychologists who promote permissiveness.[20] However, psychology gets the credit even though that principle has been around ever since Adam and Eve. There are numerous examples in the Old Testament where principles of disciplining in love are stated and developed. Also, Ephesians 6:4 instructs fathers to bring up their children in the nurture and admonition of the Lord. Although Dobson uses Scripture to give his points added strength, many of his teachings glorify the psychological wisdom of the world more than the God of the Bible. But, that is to be expected. After all, he is a licensed psychologist. **He believes in psychology and that is the position of authority from which he teaches.**

When Dobson says something that seems true about child rearing, the impression one gets is that he gleaned it from psychology rather than the Bible. For instance, in *Dare to*

Discipline, instead of giving the reader God's Word on the matter of love and discipline, he quotes a psychologist. He says:

> At a recent psychologists' conference in Los Angeles, the keynote speaker made the statement that *the greatest social disaster of this century is the belief that abundant love makes discipline unnecessary.*[21](Emphasis his.)

It's great that a psychologist realized and admitted the mistake that many other psychologists make. On the other hand, God's Word was clear on this issue a long time ago. For example, Proverbs 29:15 clearly says, "The rod and reproof give wisdom: but a child left to himself bringeth his mother to shame." Little is said about God's authority and God's Word on the matter. The question being asked is not "What does the Bible say about this?" Instead we find out what psychology says on the matter, or at least what some psychologists may be saying for a while. Furthermore, when individual psychologists make pronouncements, they do not represent all psychologists or all systems of psychology. They only represent the opinions of one or more of them.

In spite of the disagreement and the lack of scientific support, Dobson and other psychologists speak as experts and authorities even though they are merely offering opinions. The only authoritative source of information about the human condition and matters of life and godliness is the Bible. And yet in most of his books, little appeal is given to the Bible, and even statements that could have biblical support are made as though they came out of psychological investigation. An example of a very good statement Dobson makes is:

> Respectful and responsible children result from families where the proper combination of *love and discipline* is present. [22] (Emphasis his.)

But, rather than giving biblical support for the statement, Dobson merely states it from his assumed position of an

authority in child development. And, indeed, he very well could
have learned this in his psychology classes. Even some secularists have opposed permissiveness and noticed the effects of
combining love and discipline. However, the only way we can
know that what they have observed is true is by checking to see
if the principle is found in the Bible. But, if it is already in the
Bible, why not study the Bible to learn about human behavior
rather than psychology?

In presenting his five key elements for properly controlling
children in *Dare to Discipline,* he says, *"Developing respect for
the parents is the critical factor in child management."*[23]
(Emphasis his.) Here again he does not state this as God's
Word to parents and children, even though honoring parents is
one of the Ten Commandments. The appeal is not for parents
to obey God and to teach their children to obey God. Instead, he
gives reasons related to results.

From the perspective of psychology, Dobson advises parents
to let children learn from the consequences of their own
actions. But, one does not need psychological training to know
that people can learn from the consequences of their behavior.
That wisdom is taught throughout all of Scripture. It is the
kind of wisdom that has been passed on from generation to
generation for centuries without the help of psychology. It is
part of the admonition to older women in Paul's letter to
Titus—to teach the younger women. But since people in our
culture look primarily to professionals for advice, they think
that even ordinary, everyday advice must come from some kind
of worldly "expert."

Dobson offers suggestions for parents to love their children
in practical ways. However, the goal is generally to build the
child's self-esteem rather than simply to obey God and nurture
children for Christ's sake and service. In fact, Dobson majors in
self-esteem teachings which have their roots in secular humanistic psychology.

In addition to crediting psychology as being a source of
knowledge for knowing how to live and how to rear children,
Dobson substitutes Mother Nature for God the Creator in his

opening paragraph of the first chapter of *Dare to Discipline*. One tends to overlook the replacement because of Dobson's folksy way of telling the story about the frog who stayed in the pot while the water was slowly heated to boiling. However, it matches his tendency to subsume Scripture with psychology in areas where the Lord has clearly spoken.

Dobson uses the story of the frog that did not sense his danger to illustrate the plight of parents who are blind to problems that gradually build until they reach a boiling point. But, the same story also illustrates the plight of the church in which psychological theories and pronouncements about the condition of man and how he should live are eroding the faith once delivered unto the saints. While Christians recognize the dangers of obvious occultism and competing faith systems and cults, they do not realize the gradual substitution of the opinions of men in place of the Word of God.

Dobson's books emphasize his brand of psychology instead of the Word of God. And while there may be some points of apparent agreement between certain ideas in psychology and the Bible, psychology rather than the Bible is the authority for too much of what Dobson says and writes. He has elected to look to psychology for answers and he speaks from that source, even though any good, useful advice, while having been collected, categorized, and claimed by psychology, has been around for centuries. Nevertheless, readers pay attention to what Dobson says because he is a psychologist. They forget how long real wisdom has been around.

3

Dr. Dobson's Commitment to Psychology

Today, the influence of psychology is not limited to Christians of liberal persuasion, nor is it limited to those of neo-orthodox persuasion, nor is it confined within denominational boundaries. The influence of psychological theories having to do with understanding the nature of man and with matters of life and conduct has crossed the boundary of every denomination and even reaches its tentacles around those attempting to remain true to the fundamentals of the Christian faith.

Psychological counselors who are also professing Christians contend that the Bible does not speak to every situation and therefore needs certain supplementation or integration with so-called psychological truths, which are simply the opinions of men based upon limited, often very subjective information. There is an assumption that psychological theories contain truths that the Bible somehow missed.

Dobson's faith in psychology can be seen throughout his books. He quotes numerous psychologists as authorities and recommends their books. Among the psychologists he cites authoritatively are Sigmund Freud,[1] B.F. Skinner,[2] E.L. Thorndike,[3] William Glasser,[4] Stanley Coopersmith,[5] and Clyde Narramore.[6] Throughout his books he recommends professional counseling. Moreover, Focus on the Family has become a vast referral system for Christians to be therapized by professional, psychologically-trained counselors.

The staff at Focus on the Family refers those seeking a counselor to licensed therapists only. This excludes pastoral counselors who do not hold those degrees and licenses which require extensive course work in psychology. Since the Focus on the Family policy is to refer only to licensed counselors, anyone who relies solely on the Word of God and work of the Holy Spirit need not apply. Therefore, if a person requests the name of a Christian counselor, he will be referred to a professing Christian who is trained in psychological notions and methods.

Dobson recommends professional counseling and vividly describes what he believes to be the ideal therapeutic relationship in his book *Hide or Seek*. The therapist is portrayed as savior. And the thrust of humanistic psychology can be seen in the sentimental unconditional acceptance that Carl Rogers equated with love. Dobson dramatizes the supposed internal response of the client and then equates professional psychological counseling with the essence of biblical compassion and with the biblical commandment to "bear one another's burdens."[7] Of course no mention is made about the exchange of money for "professional services." Nor does he mention that Paul would not equate bearing one another's burdens (Gal. 6:2) with psychological counseling. Indeed, in Galatians 6 the counseling is spiritual and can only be done by those who are spiritual. Paul's epistle to the Galatians explicitly warns against Christians following or dispensing other gospels built upon the vain philosophies of men rather than established by the cross of Christ and the Word of God.

While Dobson says that he rejected some of what he learned in psychology classes, he contends that "there are many instances where traditional psychological understandings are perfectly consistent with biblical teaching."[8] Therefore he encourages young people to consider psychology as their vocation. He says:

Psychology offers a unique opportunity for a person to be of service as a disciple of Christ. . . . I have found it rewarding in my practice to represent the Christian view of marriage, morality, parenting, and honesty, while respecting the right of the individual to make his own choice. What I'm saying is that Christian psychology is a worthy profession for a young believer to pursue, *provided* his own faith is strong enough to withstand the humanistic concepts to which he will be exposed in graduate school.[9] (Emphasis his.)

Then he cautions: "If he begins to compromise on his fundamental beliefs, he could easily become a liability and a hindrance to the Christian faith."[10] However, Dobson's note of caution is not strong enough. In order to become a disciple of Christ in a career of counseling psychology, one must also be a disciple of such psychologists as Freud, Skinner, Adler, Fromm, Maslow, and Rogers. The compromise is so subtle that those who call themselves Christian psychologists do not realize the extent to which they allow psychological presuppositions to compromise their faith. However, each concession to psychology eats away at total reliance on God and His Word until psychology is no longer a supplement to the Bible, but a supplanter of the Word. Soon the dominant perspective on human nature is psychological rather than biblical.

The Psychological Perspective

Our culture has come to view problems of living psychologically. Rather than looking at problems from a biblical viewpoint, many Christians have also come to perceive problems from a psychological perspective. A good example of this is the opening illustration of Dobson's book *Hide or Seek: How to Build Self-Esteem in Your Child.* In his graphic storytelling mode, Dobson says:

He began his life with all the classic handicaps and disadvantages. His mother was a powerfully built, dominating woman who found it difficult to love anyone.[11]

Dobson proceeds to tell about her lack of affection, love, and discipline and about the rejection the young man had experienced throughout his life. He tells about the boy's school failures, how he was laughed at and ridiculed in the Marines, how he therefore resisted authority, and how he was dishonorably discharged. Dobson continues the pathetic story of this supposed victim of circumstances with "no sense of worthiness."[12] Then, after describing the man's bad marriage, Dobson writes:

No one wanted him. No one had ever wanted him. He was perhaps the most rejected man of our time. His ego lay shattered in a fragmented dust! [13]

Near the end of the story, the man's identity is revealed. He was President Kennedy's assassin. Dobson concludes:

Lee Harvey Oswald, the rejected, unlovable failure, killed the man who, more than any other man on earth, embodied all the success, beauty, wealth, and family affection which he lacked. In firing that rifle, he utilized the *one* skill he had learned in his entire, miserable lifetime.[14] (Emphasis his.)

Dobson wrote the story of Lee Harvey Oswald to make a strong point concerning feelings of inferiority and low self-esteem that Dobson believes are rampant among youth. He concludes the story with these words:

Thus, much of the rebellion, discontent, and hostility of the teen-age years emanates from overwhelming, uncontrollable feelings of inferiority and inadequacy which rarely find verbal expression.[15]

Dobson's description of Oswald's life reveals a psychological viewpoint influenced by underlying ideologies of the Freudian unconscious, Adlerian inferiority, and the humanistic belief in the intrinsic goodness of man and the universal victimization of the individual by parents and society. The culprit is society (mainly parents) and the diagnosis is low self-esteem with feelings of inferiority and inadequacy. In fact, those feelings are presented as overwhelming and uncontrollable and thus causing rebellion. Therefore the universal solution to personal problems, rebellion, unhappiness, and hostility presented throughout Dobson's books is raising self-esteem.

Beginning with a reconstruction of Lee Harvey Oswald's life presented in a contemporary psychological framework, Dobson sets the stage for psychological explanations of problems of living and psychological solutions. How one sees a problem will determine the solutions offered. Dobson graphically sets forth Oswald as a victim of deep feelings of inferiority, self-hatred, and low self-esteem caused by a domineering mother who did not cherish her child and a society which did not value him.

While Dobson is careful to say that Oswald must still be held responsible for his criminal behavior,[16] the thrust of the story emphasizes a kind of psychic determinism which led to his horrendous crime. In other words, Oswald is seen as a victim of circumstances and society. The emphasis in the story is about Oswald's unfulfilled needs for love, acceptance, and worth rather than about the horror of the actions he chose. He is presented more as a victim of internal and external forces than as a sinner in need of a savior.

Of course the primary point Dobson dramatizes is that if a person develops feelings of inferiority and low self-esteem he will have a miserable life, which could lead in the same disastrous direction as Oswald's. He says:

> The greater tragedy is that Lee Harvey Oswald's plight is not unusual in America today. While others may respond less aggressively, this same consuming awareness of inadequacy can be seen in every avenue of life.[17]

Therefore, the preventive medicine for society which Dobson presents throughout *Hide or Seek* is strategies for developing self-esteem and self-worth.

The Psychological View or the Biblical View?

Psychological solutions often seem to make sense when the problem is presented from a psychological viewpoint. However, is there possibly another way for Christians to look at such a life of misery and violence? What if the story had been written from a biblical, Christian perspective? One might say that the boy was born to a godless woman who neither cared for God nor for His gift of a child, a woman who exhibited the works of the flesh rather than the fruit of the Spirit, who herself had either never heard of or else rebelled against the Gospel of Jesus Christ, who was her only hope of salvation. Thus she brought up her son in the same sinful manner in which she herself lived, rather than in the nurture and admonition of the Lord. Rather than teaching him the Love of God through words and actions, she taught him her own evil ways of rebellion, blame, frustration, despair, and hopelessness. One might conclude that since she did not know the Savior, she was her own god, pursuing her own will and not caring a whit for others. Doesn't the Bible tell us about such a life lived according to the sin nature? (See, for example, Romans 1:21-32 and Eph. 4:17-19.)

Then as Oswald continued his life in this world, he also depended upon his own flesh. His life seems to parallel Paul's description of the Gentiles, as being "without Christ, being aliens from the commonwealth of Israel [in this case separated from the household of faith], and strangers from the covenants of promise, having no hope, and without God in the world" (Eph. 2:12). Evidently at no time in his life did he believe the Gospel and receive new life, for true faith in Jesus **does** transform a person's life from darkness into light, from despair to hope, from alienation into a love relationship that surpasses even the best that parents can give.

If the story is told in the context of Scripture, both the analysis and the answers will come from an understanding of the law of God and the Gospel of Jesus Christ. In short, the sinful self and its activities are recognized as the problem, not just as a generalized conclusion, but as a careful analysis. And, the solution is Jesus Christ, not just as a catch-all phrase, but as the living reality of the full effect of the cross, of the resurrection, and of "Christ in you, the hope of glory."

If most Christians truly believed this, they would double their efforts toward evangelism and discipleship. More would reach out to those who have been going the way of the world, the flesh and the devil with both the truth of God and the mercy of God. More would be on fire for the Gospel. Instead, however, too many have been enticed by many other gospels offered by psychology and by those professing Christians who promote the psychological way.

Unfortunately, however, these essential truths have become relegated to the "of-course-we-all-know-that-but" category. They are looked upon as old fashioned thinking and old fashioned terminology. In subtle ways the Bible is put on the back burner, and many in the church are cooking with popular psychologies instead of the Word of God. Rather than the solutions to life's problems coming from God's plan for mankind as outlined in His Word, the solutions come from secular psychological theories.

Dobson views problems of living from a psychological perspective. In fact he contends that both Oswald and the other Kennedy assassin, Sirhan Sirhan, followed these steps to destruction:

> (1) they experienced deep-seated feelings of inferiority; (2) they sought to cope by withdrawal and surrender; (3) their vain attempts to achieve adequacy were miserable failures; and (4) they exploded in violence.[18]

Again, this is a combination of Alfred Adler's theories about inferiority, Sigmund Freud's unconscious defense mechanisms, and the defunct hydraulic model of energy theory. Dobson calls this last theory a "psychological law." He says:

> Remember this psychological law: any anxiety-producing thought or condition which cannot be expressed is almost certain to generate inner pressure and stress.[19]

In his book *Emotions: Can You Trust Them?* Dobson dramatically asserts:

> When *any* powerful emotion is forced from conscious thought while it is raging full strength, it has the potential of ripping and tearing us from within. The process by which we cram a strong feeling into the unconscious mind is called "repression," and it is psychologically hazardous. The pressure that it generates will usually appear elsewhere in the form of depression, anxiety, tension, or in an entire range of physical disorders.[20] (Emphasis his.)

Researchers refer to this particular notion as the hydraulic model of emotions. The model says simply that if emotional energy is blocked in one place it must be released elsewhere. However, this is only an opinion. It is not a "psychological law" or a psychological fact. Researcher Dr. Carol Tavris says, "Today the hydraulic model of energy has been scientifically discredited."[21] Nevertheless psychologists tend to expand the hydraulic idea to all emotions in spite of the opposing research. Therefore Dobson's "psychological law" is merely his Freudian opinion, which has been scientifically discredited.

In the opening chapter of *Hide or Seek* Dobson uses a psychological foundation and framework for defining, diagnosing, and solving problems of living. He describes problems in psychological rather than biblical terms. Then, he analyzes problems according to what parents and society did not provide in terms of so-called needs of the self as proposed by humanistic psychology. His solutions or goals are self-esteem and self-confidence. And the rest of the book is devoted to strategies for overcoming the problem (low-self esteem and inferiority) through building high self-esteem and self-confidence.

But, if we are going to believe in the sufficiency of God's Word for matters of life and godliness, we need to evaluate problems according to a biblical, rather than a psychological, framework. We need to ask the following questions. Will our description of problems be in psychological rather than biblical language? Will we analyze problems according to ideologies behind the psychologies, such as tenets of secular humanism, psychic or environmental determinism, the so-called unconscious, or behaviorism? Or will we analyze the problem according to God's Word? Will our solutions and goals be based upon psychological theories (such as in Dobson's illustration) and the so-called hierarchy of needs (including the need for self-esteem)? Or will our solutions and goals be biblical ones? Will we look to human strategies for overcoming the problems identified by Dobson as low-self esteem and inferiority? Or will we trust God's ways of transforming sinners into saints through His Word and His Spirit, thereby enabling Christians to walk according to the spirit rather than the flesh?

The Religion of Pragmatism

The influence of pragmatism among Christians cannot be overestimated. The crux of the matter is this: Will we obey God because He is God or will we obey God **if** we think that it will work for our own good? The quick response of most Christians is, "Of course we will obey God because He is God." Nevertheless, most appeals to Christians are based on the premise that something works and is good for someone. These goals can be confused because God's will is indeed best for us. But, when the reason shifts from God's authority to whether something works for my best interests, then I have fallen for pragmatism.

In attempting to avoid a dogmatic, authoritarian manner of presenting the Word of God, many Christian speakers and writers supply man-centered reasons for obeying God. It is a subtle shift, which places man's opinion of what is good above what God has said is right and good. It is the same philosophical and ethical stance that prevailed during the time of Judges.

> In those days there was no king in Israel, but every man did that which was right in his own eyes. (Judges 17:6 and 21:25.)

Just as that was the pathetic condition during the period of Judges, this seems to be the hallmark of our present age and the church has not been immune to its influence. Just before that pathetic period Joshua had declared: "As for me and my house, we will serve the Lord." And while Dobson may sincerely believe that his message resembles Joshua's, his reliance on pragmatism taints his message with the humanistic ethic based on what looks right, whether through the eyes of a single person or through the eyes of psychological observers of behavior.

Dobson's advice in *What Wives Wish Their Husbands Knew About Women* is based more on pragmatism than on God's will. For instance, Dobson describes what he calls "a universal characteristic of human nature" and then talks about how women can use this to their advantage. He says:

> *We value that which we are fortunate to get; we discredit that with which we are stuck! We lust for the very thing which is beyond our grasp; we disdain the same item when it becomes a permanent possession.* [22](Emphasis his.)

He follows this with a discussion about how women can use this to manipulate relationships. He illustrates that by saying how he used an attitude of self confidence, self respect and independence to win his wife. He then restates the formula, *"we crave that which we can't attain, but we disrespect that which we can't escape,"* and declares that "this axiom is particularly relevant in romantic matters."[23]

Even though Dobson says that he is not recommending any "sneaky cat and mouse game to recreate a 'challenge,'"[24] this kind of suggestion can very easily lead to manipulation and game playing rather than commitment to serve and obey God. His recommendation sounds like the usual advice to the lovelorn: Be "quietly confident, independent and mysterious."[25] We know this is the wisdom of the world. What would be the wisdom of God on the matter? When fear of man (or fear of losing a man) takes precedence over fear of God, worldly wisdom replaces the wisdom of God. These kinds of games prevail in the world. One would think that a Christian adviser would be more biblical in his counsel to women.

Dobson's pragmatic appeal can be seen throughout his work. His apparent reason for teaching parents to discipline their children is that it works. He quotes Jack London's words: "The best measurement of anything should be: does it work?"[26] The reason is pragmatism. And, although he brings God into the picture by saying that properly applied discipline will help teach our children about God, he does not give God's will as the primary reason for disciplining children. Elsewhere he says:

> The most magnificent theory ever devised for the control of behavior is called the "Law of Reinforcement," formulated many years ago by the first educational psychologist, E. L. Thorndike. **This is magnificent because it works!**[27] (Emphasis added.)

He says, "Good discipline is brought about by the intelligent application of this principle of reinforcement." [28] Dobson has great confidence in the Thorndike Law of Reinforcement, which he quotes: "Behavior which achieves desirable consequences will recur."[29] To illustrate the usefulness of reinforcement, Dobson tells how marvelously well this Law of Reinforcement worked on his dog. That makes sense, because Thorndike was an animal psychologist, best known for his work in animal learning. He developed the "law of effect" and is in the same tradition as behaviorists Ivan Pavlov and John B.

Watson. Such behaviorism views humans as highly evolved animals. The book *Theories of Personality* refers to Thorndike's law of effect as a "hedonistic formulation."[30]

Dobson evidently believes that what works with dogs will work with humans. In other words, he is recommending that, when it comes to training and discipline, parents treat their children like animals. Dobson declares: "Rewards are not only useful in shaping animal behavior; they succeed even better with humans."[31] He comes to his conclusions regarding rewards from animal psychology rather than from the Bible.

Dobson then presents this psychological theory as fact:

> It is an absolute fact that unreinforced behavior will eventually disappear. This process, called *extinction* by psychologists, can be very useful to parents and teachers who want to alter the characteristics of children.[32]

While this may be true of animals it is not always true of people. Because of the complexity of sinful humanity and because other factors enter in, one cannot say categorically, "It is an absolute fact that. . . ." In fact, many people get stuck in unproductive activities that continue in spite of adverse results.

Jay Adams disagrees with Dobson's behavioristic methods of training children. He says:

> James Dobson's book *Dare to Discipline* . . . while placing a needed emphasis upon discipline by structure, is based upon this non-Christian ideology. It is basically a godless humanistic book. The discipline advocated is behavioristic (Skinnerian). According to Dobson, a child is to be "trained" as one would train his dog. The methodology does not differ. The presupposition (not stated, but underlying the book) is that man is but another animal. There is no place for the work of the Holy Spirit in conversion or sanctification. Change takes place strictly on the horizontal level.[33]

Adams also says:

> When Dobson, for instance, recommends strictly behavioristic methods for child raising *in the name of Christianity*, he badly confuses important distinctions and erases lines that forever must be drawn clearly. His near total capitulation to behaviorism is couched in Christian terms but really introduces an equally godless system into the Christian home while purporting to be a Christian reaction to permissiveness. . . . Conspicuously absent in such child discipline is the use of the Scriptures, conversion, repentance, the work of the Holy Spirit, and sanctification. Ephesians 6:4 emphasizes, in contrast, *both* discipline (by reward and punishment) and nouthetic confrontation (the "nurture *and* admonition of the Lord").[34] (Emphasis his.)

Rather than using the Bible to discover God's principle of reward and punishment and of mercy and justice, Dobson turns to psychological behaviorism and credits Skinner, Thorndike *et al.* for giving parents the wherewithal to discipline their children. And, of course, the appeal to parents is that **it works.**

Why should Christians follow a course of action? Because it works or because it is God's will? The origin of any teaching will determine the direction it goes. If parents discipline their children according to his Word and because God requires it, they are responding in obedience to God and the direction will be towards God. If, on the other hand, parents discipline their children according to the opinions of men because they work, the direction is too often towards self. Parents can feel good about themselves, and children can feel good about themselves, but will they truly submit to God's will even when obedience doesn't look as if it's working to their benefit?

The crux of the matter is this: Are we to do what God says even when we do not see results? Or are we to say that something is right and good because it works? Will we follow pragmatism or biblical authority? Pragmatism may very well come from and lead to love of self, while obedience to God comes from and leads to love for God. The danger of pragmatism is that one may be doing right things for wrong reasons. Goals and values become secularized and person-centered rather than sacred and God-centered.

On the other hand, a number of parents who use some of Dobson's advice may actually be following biblical authority because they know what God has said on the matter. If obedience to God is the motivation rather than pragmatism, they may very well be pleasing God and having success. But, if the motive is for success and because it works, they may become discouraged when it doesn't work and try something else.

Pragmatism must not be the primary reason even for obedience to God. However, obedience to God does work to bring us closer to Him and to mold us into the image of Christ. Nevertheless, love for God, rather than pragmatism, must be the reason for whatever we do in raising our children, as well as for whatever we think or do in all areas of our lives.

Dobson's Criticisms of Psychology

Although Dobson demonstrates commitment to the psychological way of understanding people and helping them, he voices strong criticism of those psychological theories and techniques he does not agree with. This is not unusual. With over 450 different systems of psychotherapy (psychological counseling) and the often contradictory theories of child psychology, there is bound to be conflict. Rather than each so-called discovery and theory adding to a cohesive body of knowledge, psychology is made up of a cacophony of conflicting voices. To add to the confusion, psychologists are often eclectic. Each one picks and chooses bits and pieces he happens to like. Therefore, each psychologist offers his own concoction.

Dobson's primary area of study was child development, which is concerned with how children learn and develop through their ages and stages. It studies how children process information, how they learn, what they like to do, what they can do, in short, what is natural for them at any particular age. This field of study is dominated by professional educators and psychologists who are now the so-called experts, who speak as authorities even though they are often merely voicing their own opinions and biases. Although the study of child development and educational psychology have some basis in objective observation, they are not free from contamination. They are filled with subjectivity and are contaminated with presuppositions which conflict with the Bible, including evolutionism, behaviorism, pragmatism, and humanism.

Dobson opposes the teachings of certain authorities in his own field. Because every psychologist must choose from the various conflicting theories, each psychologist inevitably ends up, as Dobson does, disagreeing with other psychologists. Dobson rightly criticizes his colleagues who promote permissiveness. He declares that permissiveness is based upon the presuppositions that people are born good and that if they are allowed to develop with as little interference as possible they will become wonderful people. The presupposition is wrong.

But even though Dobson objects to that presupposition of secular humanism as it relates to permissiveness, his own promotion of self-esteem comes from the same source. Self-esteem teachings come from humanistic psychologists who presuppose that people are born good and that when their needs for self-worth, self-esteem, and self-actualization are met they will be good people who are socially responsible. Dobson picks from the same tree as the promoters of permissiveness and offers the fruit to fellow Christians.

Dobson's Criticisms of Experts

Although his authoritative position in Christendom depends upon his status as a licensed psychologist and an expert in child development, Dobson also expresses his concern about people depending upon "experts." While parents of past generations learned about child rearing from members of their extended family, he says that parents now look to experts because they feel unprepared for raising children. Therefore they "have turned to pediatricians, psychologists, psychiatrists and educators for answers to their questions about the complexities of parenthood."[35] He continues:

> Therefore, increasing numbers of American children have been reared according to this professional consultation during the past forty years. In fact, no country on earth has embraced the teachings of child psychology and the offerings of family specialists more than has the United States.[36]

Those psychologists, educational psychologists, and psychiatrists are the very ones who have undermined parents and made them feel inadequate and dependent upon "experts." Freud created much criticism of parents and doubt about their expertise. He and numerous other psychological "experts" have nearly destroyed the thread of passing wisdom from one generation to another through the family.

Although Dobson is part of the group of "experts" who have intimidated parents, he asks: "What has been the effect of this professional influence?" Then, in answer to his own question, he bemoans the rise of "delinquency, drug abuse, alcoholism, unwanted pregnancies, mental illness, and suicide" among young people. He declares: "In many ways, we have made a mess of parenthood!"[37] And while he is careful not to place the entire blame on psychologists, he says:

> I believe they [the professional "experts"] have played a role in creating the problem. Why? *Because in general, behavioral scientists have lacked confidence in the Judeo-Christian ethic and have disregarded the wisdom of this priceless tradition.* [38](Emphasis his.)

We agree with his criticism of the substitution of the psychological opinions of men for what he calls the "Judeo-Christian ethic," though we would be more specific and use the entire Word of God, rather than a "Judeo-Christian ethic," which is looser in definition and practice.

Dobson criticizes members of his own profession for ignoring wisdom from the past and "substituting instead their own wobbly-legged insights of the moment."[39] We agree with his description of the substitution, but it is even more serious when Christians ignore the Word of God and substitute the "wobbly-legged insights" of psychological opinions. And we thoroughly agree with his next remark about psychological "experts":

> Each authority, writing from his own limited experience and reflecting his own unique biases, has sold us his guesses and suppositions as though they represented Truth itself.[40]

Dobson bemoans the anti-Christian bias of secular psychologists who "have argued God out of existence."[41] Lest anyone misunderstand him, however, Dobson is quick to defend his own position. He places himself outside those psychologists who depend upon the wrong source for wisdom in dealing with the issues and problems of life. He says:

> How do my writings differ from the unsupported recommendations of those whom I have criticized? The distinction lies in the *source* of the views being presented. The underlying principles expressed herein are not my own innovative insights which would be forgotten in a brief season or two. Instead, they originated with the inspired biblical writers who gave us the foundation for all relationships in the home.[42] (Emphasis his.)

This is an extremely important point which requires examination. We know that Dobson thinks that his source is the Bible, and yet the Bible does not teach a number of concepts that Dobson teaches. And while some of his teachings may agree with the Bible, psychology plays a significant role in his teachings—so much so that we would venture to say that Dobson's source for much of what he teaches is the very psychological cistern he criticizes: humanistic psychology with its hierarchy of needs, including the so-called needs for self-esteem, self-worth and self-confidence. And while his emphasis on love and discipline sound very biblical, behavioral psychology and pragmatism are strong contenders as the underlying source.

Dobson is right in not trying to take credit for his ideas as though he himself discovered them, because they are not simply his own "innovative insights." They are taken from the insights of secular psychological theorists and given a biblical boost. He says that his purpose in writing has been "nothing more ambitious than to verbalize the Judeo-Christian tradition regarding discipline of children and to apply those concepts to today's families."[43] But Dobson's "Judeo-Christian tradition" can hardy be distinguished from traditional American middle-class family values and is vague enough to incorporate any psychological notions he wishes to promote.

Because he chose to "verbalize" a tradition rather than a solidly biblical Christianity, Dobson gave himself latitude to include unholy mixtures of the wisdom of the world, the tradition of men, and enough Bible to lend authority and appeal to his Christian sensibilities. Terms such as *Judeo-Christian tradition* and *Judeo-Christian ethic*, while loosely attached to Old Testament law, designate something quite different from Christianity. For instance Judaism and Christianity do **not** agree on many things, including the source of change and help (Christ's death and resurrection) or its power (the indwelling Holy Spirit). It is to the whole counsel of God we must turn.

4

Self-Etc.

The concept of self-esteem dominates Dobson's work. Self-esteem, with its entourage of other self-hyphenated words, permeates his teaching. It began in his first book, came to full bloom in his second book, and serves as a major presupposition throughout the rest of his writing and speaking. In *Dare to Discipline* he says:

> Self-esteem is the most fragile attribute in human nature; it can be damaged by a very minor incident and its reconstruction is often difficult to engineer.[1]

The major theme and purpose of Dobson's book *Hide or Seek: How to Build Self-Esteem in Your Child* is increasing self-esteem. He says:

> It has been my purpose to formulate a well-defined philosophy—an approach to child rearing—which will contribute to self-esteem from infancy onward.[2]

One of his primary objectives for *What Wives Wish Their Husbands Knew about Women* is to: "Point the pathway toward greater self-esteem and acceptance."[3] For Dobson self-esteem, self-worth, self-acceptance and their related self-words are crucial, not only for the individual but for the society as well. He contends that:

> **... low self-esteem is a threat to the entire human family, affecting children, adolescents, the elderly, all socioeconomic levels of society, and each race and ethnic culture.**[4] (Emphasis added.)

As with most promoters of self-esteem, Dobson equates low self-esteem with feelings of inadequacy, inferiority, self-doubt, and an inadequate sense of personal worth. He continues his litany of woe for a society which does not do all it can to increase personal worth and self-esteem. He says:

> The matter of personal worth is not only the concern of those who lack it. In a real sense, the health of an entire society depends on the ease with which its individual members can gain personal acceptance. *Thus, whenever the keys to self-esteem are seemingly out of reach for a large percentage of the people, as in the twentieth-century America, then widespread "mental illness," neuroticism, hatred, alcoholism, drug abuse, violence, and social disorder will certainly occur. Personal worth is not something human beings are free to take or leave. We must have it, and when it is unattainable, everybody suffers* [5] (Emphasis his.)

Dobson contends that social problems are the direct result of people unsuccessfully trying to deal with inferiority, or feelings of self-doubt. He has even named a law after himself. "Dobson's Law" says:

> When the incidence of self-doubt is greatest, accompanied by the unavailability of acceptable solutions, then the probability of irresistible social disorder is maximized.[6]

He further declares, "Inferiority even motivates wars and international politics."[7] In fact, he attributes the attempted genocide of the Jews in Germany to an inferiority complex.[8] Things get reversed when discussing inferiority. Suddenly, the most egotistical people are excused with a diagnosis of inferiority. It begins to sound like Isaiah's prophecy:

> Woe unto them that call evil good, and good evil; that put darkness for light and light for darkness; that put bitter for sweet, and sweet for bitter. Woe unto them that are wise in their own eyes, and prudent in their own sight (Isaiah 5:20-21).

Not only that, Dobson declares that inferiority feelings are "the major force behind the rampaging incidence of rape today."[9] Thus low self-esteem is viewed as the cause of all kinds of problems, and high self-esteem is considered to be an absolute necessity for survival.

The issue of self-esteem is not a peripheral issue with Dobson. It is central to all he teaches about children, adults, and society. It is such a foundational assumption for him that it permeates all of his other work. Thus, in order to evaluate Dobson's work it is necessary to examine the source of self-esteem teachings and to compare those teachings with God's Holy Word.

The Genesis of Self-Esteem

The present self-esteem movement has its most recent roots in clinical psychology, namely in the personality theories of such men as William James, Alfred Adler, Erich Fromm, Abraham Maslow, and Carl Rogers. It became further popularized by their many followers, including Stanley Coopersmith, Nathaniel Brandon, and California Assemblyman John Vasconcellos. Nevertheless the roots of the self-esteem movement reach further back into human history.

The self-esteem movement began in the third chapter of Genesis. Initially Adam and Eve were God-conscious and aware of one another and their surroundings rather than being self-conscious. Their awareness of themselves was incidental and peripheral to their focus on God and one another. Adam realized that Eve was bone of his bone and flesh of his flesh, but he was not self-aware in the same sense that his descendants would be. Self was not the issue until the Fall.

The one and only restriction in the Garden of Eden was that which would lead Adam and Eve into a new mode of self-awareness. The forbidden fruit from the tree of the knowledge of good and evil birthed a sinful self that would seek fulfillment and gratification. The tempter seduced Eve away from trusting God's love and into trusting self and Satan. The serpent slyly asked, "Yea, hath God said, Ye shall not eat of every tree of the garden?" Then as soon as he saw that Eve was open to doubting the absolute truth of God, he boldly contradicted God's Word by saying, "Ye shall not surely die" (Genesis 3:1, 3). Next he implied that God was withholding good from her by saying:

> For God doth know that in the day ye eat thereof, then your eyes shall be opened, and ye shall be as gods, knowing good and evil (Genesis 3:4).

Thus God's Word and His love were undermined, and Eve took the first step in the direction of self-love, self-gratification and self-fulfillment.

> And when the woman saw that the tree was good for food, and that it was pleasant to the eyes, and a tree to be desired to make one wise, she took of the fruit thereof, and did eat, and gave also unto her husband with her; and he did eat (Genesis 3:6).

Here was the first offer to become self-actualized. Rather than waiting on God in trust and obedience, Eve decided to satisfy herself. This was the beginning of loving self more than

God. This was the beginning of esteeming self more than God. And this was the beginning of having greater confidence in self than in God—this was the genesis of self as god.

Adam and Eve were suddenly aware of themselves in a new way.

> And the eyes of them both were opened, and they knew that they were naked; and they sewed fig leaves together, and made themselves aprons (Genesis 3:7).

They not only became aware of themselves; they became self-conscious. Their immediate response was to cover themselves with leaves. Rather than looking at God, they looked at themselves. Instead of reflecting God, they formed their own self-image. The image of God was obscured by an image of self.

Although their eyes were opened, self-awareness did not bring enlightenment, as twentieth-century psychology proposes. Instead it was the beginning of the darkness spoken of by Paul when he described how the Gentiles walk, "in the vanity of their mind, having the understanding darkened, being alienated from the life of God through the ignorance that is in them, because of the blindness of their heart" (Ephesians 4:17, 18). And it all began with a focus on self.

Partaking of the tree of the knowledge of good and evil did not bring godly wisdom. It brought guilt, fear, and separation from God. Thus, when Adam and Eve heard God approaching, they hid in the bushes. But God saw them and asked, "Who told thee that thou wast naked? Hast thou eaten of the tree, whereof I commanded thee that thou shouldest not eat?" (Genesis 3:11).

Adam and Eve answered with the first example of self-justification. First Adam blamed Eve and God, and then Eve blamed the serpent. The fruit of the knowledge of good and evil spawned the sinful self with all of its self-love, self-esteem, self-acceptance, self-justification, self-righteousness, self-actualization, self-denigration, self-pity and other forms of self-focus and self-centeredness.

The present Self-Etc. movement is thus rooted in Adam and Eve's sin. Through the centuries mankind has continued to feast at the tree of the knowledge of good and evil, which has spread its branches of worldly wisdom. It has branched out into the vain philosophies of men and, more recently, the "scientized" philosophies and metaphysics of modern psychology. The four branches of psychology which seek to supplant the Word of God are the psychoanalytic, the behavioristic, the humanistic, and the transpersonal. Those kinds of psychology are neither objective nor scientific. They are bound to subjectivity and bias, built on presuppositions which often conflict with the revealed Word of God. They consist of the worldly wisdom of men, which Jesus, the prophets, and the apostles rejected (1 Corinthians 2). They are part of the world referred to in 1 John 2:

> Love not the world, neither the things that are in the world. If any man love the world, the love of the Father is not in him. For all that is in the world, the lust of the flesh, and the lust of the eyes, and the pride of life, is not of the Father, but is of the world (1 John 2:15-16).

Existentialism along with secular humanism undergirds the great emphasis on the self. Personal subjectivity and feelings are the hallmarks of existential humanism. The self is both the center and evaluator of experience and its needs must be met. Humanistic psychology has provided the justification for emphasizing the self through its hierarchy of needs for self-acceptance, self-worth, self-love, and self-actualization. Self, rather than God or others, is the central focus.

Lest this sound selfish and self-centered, the proponents of the self assure us that only through meeting the needs of the self can people become socially aware and responsive. The logic follows this pattern: only when a person loves himself can he love others; only when a person accepts himself can he accept others; and only when his needs are met can he meet the needs of others. This logic is the underlying justification for most of what goes on in humanistic psychology, and it spills over into almost every other issue of life.

Religious incantations for self-worth, self-love, and self-acceptance ooze out of the TV tube, drift across radio waves, and entice through advertising. From the cradle to the grave, self-promoters promise to cure all of society's ills through doses of self-esteem, self-worth, self-acceptance, and self-love. And everyone, or nearly everyone echoes the refrain: "You just need to love and accept yourself the way you are. You just need to forgive yourself," and "I just have to accept myself the way I am. I'm worth it. I am a lovable, valuable, forgivable person."

How is the Christian to combat the thinking of the world which glorifies the self and places self at the center as the be-all and end-all of existence? How is the Christian to be faithful to our Lord's command to be **in** the world, but not **of** the world? Can one adopt and adapt the popular philosophy/psychology of one's culture, or must one stand apart as one who has been set apart by God and view his culture by the light of the Word?

Jesus said:

> Come unto me, all ye that labour and are heavy laden, and I will give you rest. Take my yoke upon you, and learn of me; for I am meek and lowly in heart: and ye shall find rest unto your souls. For my yoke is easy, and my burden is light (Matthew 11:28-30).

Here is a call to give up one's own way and to come under the yoke of humility and service—an emphasis on yoking—on a teaching and living relationship. Jesus described His call for followers in different words, but to the same relationship and with the same intent, when He said:

> If any man will come after me, let him deny himself, and take up his cross, and follow me. For whosoever will save his life shall lose it: and whosoever will lose his life for my sake shall find it" (Matthew 16:24-25).

Jesus does not command self-love, but rather love for God and love for one another. The Bible presents an entirely different basis for love than humanistic psychology preaches. Rather than promoting self-love as the basis for loving others, the Bible says that God's love is the true source. Human love is mixed with self-love and may be ultimately self-serving. But God's love is self-giving. Therefore, when Jesus calls His disciples to deny self and to take up His yoke and His cross, He is calling them to a self-giving love, not a self-satisfying love.

Until the advent of humanistic psychology and its heavy influence in the church, Christians generally thought of self-esteem as a sinful attitude. For instance, in the fifteenth century Thomas a Kempis wrote:

> I will speak unto my Lord who am but dust and ashes. If I count myself more, behold Thou standest against me, and my iniquities bear true testimony, and I cannot gainsay it. But if I abase myself, and bring myself to nought, and shrink from all self-esteem, and grind myself to dust, which I am, thy grace will be favourable unto me, and Thy light will be near unto my heart; and all self-esteem, how little soever it be, shall be swallowed up in the depths of my nothingness, and shall perish for ever. There Thou showest to me myself, what I am, what I was, and whither I have come: *so foolish was I and ignorant* [Psalm 73:22]. If I am left to myself, behold I am nothing, I am all weakness; but if suddenly Thou look upon me, immediately I am made strong, and filled with new joy. And it is great marvel that I am so suddenly lifted up, and so graciously embraced by Thee, since I am always being carried to the deep by my own weight.[10] (Emphasis in original.)

Then in the seventeenth century Stephen Charnock wrote: "Self-esteem, self-dependence, self-willedness, is denying affection and subjection to God."[11] Arthur Pink quoted Charnock when he wrote:

Well has it been said, "To dispossess a man, then of his self-esteem and self-sufficiency, to make room for God in the heart where there was none but for sin, as dear to him as himself, to hurl down pride of nature, to make stout imaginations stoop to the cross, to make designs of self-advancement sink under a zeal for the glory of God and an overruling design for His honour, is not to be ascribed to any but to an outstretched arm wielding the sword of the Spirit."[12]

Also in the seventeenth century, Richard Baxter identified self-esteem with pride and conceit.[13] And in the nineteenth century Charles Spurgeon described the poor in spirit of the beatitudes as having "an absence of self-esteem."[14]

Lest anyone suppose that a Christian who comes face to face with the reality of his own depravity is left wallowing in the mud of his own selfhood, we must recall the context of a proper low view of self. It is in the very presence of the God of love. Jim Owen gives us a glimpse of a biblical experience of self and God:

Many believers experience a moment, I think, when the Holy Spirit brings them face to face with the biblical truth that "all have sinned and come short of the glory of God" (Romans 3:23). Overwhelmed by their vileness before the fearful and unfathomable holiness of God, so stunned by it, they sink to their knees in unutterable shame and repentance. But it does not end there. For there follows an overwhelming realization of the depth and breadth and height of God's undeserved mercy and grace given to us in Christ Jesus. So overpowering is this realization that they stay on their knees, adoring, praising and thanking God in all humility and unfeigned gratitude. For one brief moment, this side of eternity, they clearly and deeply grasp the God they worship.[15]

Then he quotes these words from a hymn by Philip Bliss:

Guilty, vile and helpless we,
Spotless lamb of God was He,
Full atonement can it be?
Hallelujah, what a Savior!

Have Christians lost sight of the grandeur of God's mercy and love? Have Christians forgotten what the cross is all about? Is that why the church is so infatuated with self-esteem and self-love?

Focus on the Self

The self has been both the subject and object of study since Eve took her first bite. The twentieth-century, however, has seen a burgeoning of open espousal of selfism. The study of the soul migrated from philosophy, metaphysics, and religion and attached itself to science and medicine. Instead of studying man from the viewpoint of the revealed Word of God, psychologists study man through subjective observation of the self and by the self. Therefore the theories they devise say more about their own subjective view of themselves and others than about mankind as a whole. The self-theorists rejected the God of the Bible as the source for their psychological doctrines of man.

Dobson's self-esteem ideas could not have originated from Scripture, because they are not there. They have been imposed on Scripture to make them palatable for Christian consumption. Nor could his self-esteem teachings have come from the history and traditions of the church before the late nineteenth century. While Dobson would not agree with all of the psychological opinions made by the such psychologists as William James, Sigmund Freud, Alfred Adler, Erich Fromm, Abraham Maslow and Carl Rogers, his self-esteem teachings have come either directly or indirectly from them.

Even though the Bible does not teach self-love, self-esteem, self-worth, or self-actualization as virtues, helps, or goals, a vast number of present-day Christians embrace the self-teachings of humanistic psychology. Rather than resisting the enticement of the world they become culture-bound. Not only do they not resist the tidal wave of selfism; they are riding the crest of self-esteem, self- acceptance, and self-love. One can hardly tell the difference between the Christian and the non-Christian in the area of the self, except that the Christian adds God as the main source for his self-esteem, self-acceptance, self-worth, and self-love.

Dobson does not stand alone. He is surrounded by a host of other psychologists and by a multitude of Christian leaders who preach self-love, self-worth, and self-esteem. While Dobson does not totally agree with all self-esteemers, he is in concert with many popular preachers of self-esteem. One is Charles Swindoll, whom Dobson quotes on certain theological issues.[16] Swindoll devotes a chapter to self-esteem in his book *Growing Wise in Family Life.*[17] In it he declares:

> A child *must* develop a good, strong self-esteem! Nothing can substitute for it. It is never automatic. The secret rests with parents who are committed to doing everything possible to make it happen.[18] (Emphasis his.)

Swindoll has evidently picked up some of his enthusiasm for self-esteem from Dobson, for he says:

> In my opinion, no one has done a better job of addressing this whole subject of struggling with self-esteem than psychologist Jim Dobson in his splendid book *Hide or Seek.* I am on my second copy and it is getting well worn. You owe it to yourself to purchase that fine volume if you are interested in coming to terms with this plaguing problem.[19]

To list the ministries and preachers who repeat the theme of self-esteem would consist of a "Who's Who" of the "big names" in the evangelical world as well as a multitude of pastors who guide their flocks to this polluted stream. With them, the so-called need for self-esteem is no longer a question. It is an assumption eroding away the very pillars of the church.

Through slogans, one-liners, and twisted Scripture, Christians jump on the existential bandwagon of humanistic psychology and set up their own cheering section. People think they'll feel better and do better if only they raise their self-esteem. Self-esteem is looked upon as a magic key to open the door to fulfillment, success, happiness, goodness, and even altruism. It is the proposed answer to nearly all problems of living. And the way it is presented it sounds good. It sounds plausible. Any criticism voiced against the teachings of self-worth, self-love, and self-esteem is regarded as *ipso facto* proof that the speaker wants people to be miserable. Moreover, any criticism against the self-esteem movement is seen as dangerous to society, since self-esteem is considered to be the panacea for its ills.

Even among Christians, self-esteem reaches a high pinnacle of moral absolutism with human need as its justification. Those humanistic psychologists who defy moral absolutism based on Scripture seduce Christians into adding a new commandment: "Thou shalt accept, esteem, love, and honor thyself." When self-love, self-acceptance, and self-esteem become moral absolutes, one can feel justified in focusing on oneself and one's own so-called psychological needs. Not only justified, but righteous!

From its secular roots self-esteem has crept into the church. It began by creeping, but now it is welcomed with open arms by many in the church who have previously attempted to stay biblical, conservative, evangelical, and fundamental. And while many attempt to modify the humanistic teachings that accompany self-esteem doctrines, the basic fundamentals of humanism cannot be divorced from self-esteem ideology.

5

Psychologized Needs, Morals, Acceptance and Forgiveness

Self-Esteem is a high-lighted buzz word of need psychology, along with the words *unconditional love*. So-called psychological needs take precedence over the explicit commands of God. The will of man, couched in terms of needs, justifies what both Christians and non-Christians want to have and do. That may sound a bit far-fetched. However, what is the appeal to Christian parents? Is it to obey the Lord in all matters of child-rearing because this is pleasing in His sight? Or is it to meet the emotional needs of the children? One may argue here that the answer is both. But, the crux of the matter is that popular programs that appeal to parents are usually based on what the child needs (according to what the child psychologists have said) rather than on what pleases God. What is the appeal of a psychologized gospel but to find religious ways to meet personal psychological needs?

Need Psychology

Many popular self-help books in Christian bookstores center on meeting personal, emotional, and relational needs.

So-called needs for self-esteem, self-love, worthwhileness, significance, and overcoming inferiority feelings dominate the thinking of many Christians. Instead of a passion for loving, obeying, and serving God in response to His Word and His love, many who name the name of Christ have turned again to meet their own so-called needs. Instead of serving as God's representatives to teach children to love and obey Him, parents have succumbed to serving their children in fear of hurting their delicate psyches.

Dobson also places a heavy emphasis on so-called needs, especially those of women and children. He stresses "unmet needs" and "emotional needs" of women.[1] He believes that "ego needs" motivate more daily behavior than anything else. He sees personal worthiness as one of those central needs, so central that he says: ". . . the human mind constantly searches and gropes for evidence of its own worthiness."[2] Thus, instead of discouraging such self-seeking, Dobson encourages women and children to believe in their own worthiness.

Dobson's message is psychological. Rather than speaking from a biblical perspective on love between man and God and between persons, Dobson parrots the secular faith in meeting needs. He quotes William Glasser as saying:

> At all times in our lives we must have at least one person who cares about us and whom we care for ourselves. If we do not have this essential person, we will not be able to fulfill our basic needs.[3]

This is not the Gospel Jesus preached. This is a secular gospel of meeting emotional needs, not a biblical Gospel of love. The focus is on me and my needs, not on God and His love and my love for him and others.

Dobson also follows the humanistic psychologists when he differentiates between how women and men meet their so-called needs for self-worth. He says that "men derive self-esteem by being *respected*; women feel worthy when they are *loved.*"[4] In fact Dobson is so certain about the importance of meeting so-called needs for self-esteem that he declares:

> If I had the power to communicate only **one message** to every family in America, I would specify the importance of **romantic love** to every aspect of feminine existence. It provides the foundation for a woman's **self-esteem**, her joy in loving, and her sexual responsiveness. Therefore, the vast number of men who are involved in bored, tired marriages—and find themselves locked out of the bedroom—should know where the trouble possibly lies. Real love can melt an iceberg.[5] (Emphasis added.)

That is quite a strong statement! If he could "communicate only one message to every family in America" it would be to "specify the importance of romantic love to every aspect of feminine existence."

Is a woman's self-esteem more important to Dobson than her salvation or sanctification? Is her self-esteem more important than her walk with God? Is "real love" necessarily romantic love? What is the purpose of that kind of love? To build a woman's self-esteem and to fulfill the husband's sexual desires? Yes, that is the "one message" Dobson would give to "every family in America."

Many Christians believe the humanistic lie that when people's needs are met, they will be good, loving people. Through the influence of humanistic psychology, they believe that people sin because their needs are not met. Some say that teenagers rebel because their needs have not been met. However, Scripture does not bear this out. Adam and Eve had it all. There was no need in their lives that was not being met to its very fullest, and yet they chose to sin, have their own way, disbelieve God, believe a lie, and love self more than God. They followed both the words and example of Satan, who as Lucifer had it all: beauty, power, authority, and all that an archangel could have and be. But Lucifer wanted to be God. And what about Israel? The more their needs were met, the less they relied on God. The more their needs were met, the more sinful they became.

And here we must distinguish between true human need, according to the Bible, and what humanistic psychologists place at the center of human need. The Bible places God's will and purpose at the center rather than so-called psychological needs. In His gracious will Jesus gives of Himself, not according to what psychologists identify as essential personal needs, but according to His perfect love and intimate knowledge of each person.

Throughout the Bible the panorama of God's plan for humanity unfolds according to His own will and purpose, which include, but go far beyond, human need. But since those psychological theories were devised by people who were seeking to understand themselves and humanity apart from God and who were looking for solutions separated from the sovereignty and will of God, their central interest was what they believed to be human need and human fulfillment without God.

Self-esteem teachings, based on the premise that self "needs" must be met before one can reach out to God and others, still end up in self. In a review of three of Dobson's books, Dr. Robert Smith notes:

> Dobson also talks about a child having a *need for self-esteem and acceptance.* These philosophies have been taught by Abraham Maslow and others who claim that they are essential prerequisites for a person to function in a responsible way. In other words, until one has these needs fulfilled, we can't expect him to obey God's commands. Again, this is unbiblical. The Word of God teaches that we must be what God wants us to be, we must obey the biblical standards at all times whether or not we have the self-esteem or acceptance or any of the other things that modern psychology might think we need. If we remember that behind every secular psychology is an unbiblical anthropology, it is easy to see how man's view of man, without God's Word, will reach such

conclusions. Unbelievers are confronting sin in man, but don't know what to do about it. But when we take a biblical view of man, we see that for the Christian the problem of man's sin has been dealt with on the cross.[6] (Emphasis his.)

From Commandments to Needs to Rights

While Christians are no longer under the law of sin and death, Jesus still calls them to obedience. He says:

This is my commandment, That ye love one another, as I have loved you (John 15:12).

Nevertheless many Christians balk at commandments unless reasons and benefits are given, and need psychology supplies them with reasons. Thus, rather than loving our children and bringing them up in the nurture and admonition of the Lord simply because God says so, we now have another reason: children need to be loved and accepted. Thus commandments have turned into needs. Worse than that, needs have replaced the commandments.

Not only have needs replaced the commandments; but the needs have also turned into rights. That is, simply being a person gives one the right to be loved. The commandment to love neighbor as self has been replaced by human rights. In our country people have a legal right to life, liberty, and the pursuit of happiness. However, since happiness is now an underlying aspect of need psychology in that people can only be happy if their emotional needs are met, the right has changed from the pursuit of happiness to the right to be happy.

Need Morality

Most Christians do not think twice when someone says that people are motivated by inner needs. Tony Walter, in his book *Need: The New Religion*, says:

It is fashionable to follow the view of some psychologists that the self is a bundle of needs and that personal growth is the business of progressively meeting these needs. Many Christians go along with such beliefs.[7]

Walter calls this obsession with needs a "new morality" and says:

> One mark of the almost total success of this new morality is that the Christian Church, traditionally keen on mortifying the desires of the flesh, on crucifying the needs of the self in pursuit of the religious life, has eagerly adopted the language of needs for itself. . . we now hear that "Jesus will meet your every need," as though he were some kind of divine psychiatrist or divine detergent, as though God were simply to service us.[8]

But Walter argues that "human need was never central to Christian theology. What was central was God's grace, not human need. True Christianity is God-centered, not man-centered."[9]

Psychological systems, however, are man-centered, not Christ-centered. They were developed as alternative ways of understanding the human condition and wrestling with problems of living. Humanistic values recast as needs replaced God's law. And somehow they seem to fit into what Dobson refers to as the Judeo-Christian ethic. Self-worth, self-esteem, and self-fulfillment are morally justified as needs. And while humanistic psychologists have removed the *ought's* and *should's* of external moral codes (such as the Bible), they have presented their own morality of needs. Walter says:

> . . . the human project as the progressive meeting of human need has been unmasked; it is a secular religion, or at least a secular morality. I suggest that atheists and agnostics who pride themselves on having dispensed with

morality and religion should ponder whether they have not let both in again through the back door.[10]

With its clarion call to self-esteem and self-worth, need psychology has the force of morality and the power of religion. But, Walter identifies this new morality and new religion as **not** compatible with Christianity. He says:

> There is one feature of some of the major writings on need that points towards need as a form of morality. Marx, Fromm, Maslow and others have noted the incompatibility between human beings orienting their lives to meeting their needs, and a traditional Christianity that would deny the needs of the self and would give charity to others not because their needs entitled them to it but out of sheer disinterested love. . . . Life as a project of meeting needs becomes almost a substitute, disguised religion.[11]

The Bible does not present self-esteem, self-worth, self-love, self-confidence, or self-fulfillment as needs that must be met to create capable, loving, well-adjusted people. Indeed the direction of Scripture is away from self and toward God and others. Self is not to be enhanced or catered to. Self-esteem is not even mentioned. On the other hand, Paul warned that a Christian is "not to think of himself more highly than he ought to think" (Romans 12:3). And when it comes to esteem, Paul says, ". . . let each esteem other better than themselves" (Philippians 2:3). From the context of Scripture, the fallen nature is already biased in the direction of self. Self love is already there or Jesus would not have commanded us to love others as we (already) love ourselves (Matthew 22:39).

Christians are not to love the world or the things of the world (1 John 2:15-16). Need psychology and the self-esteem movement are offerings of the world. And, if children and adults are encouraged to meet their so-called needs for self-esteem, self-love, self-acceptance and self-confidence, they are following the ways of the world. They fall into the sins of covetousness, envy, and pride and will not find true satisfaction. The so-called needs will always cry out because they are of the fallen nature. Christians must beware of falling back into the ways of the world and the ways of the flesh. These things are not of God even if one brings God in as the so-called source for self-esteem, self-love, self-acceptance, and self-confidence.

Jesus calls people into relationship with Himself which is so profound that He meets every true need: the need to be saved and empowered to walk in the Spirit to fulfill His will, His desire, His plan. Andrew Murray says:

> Let us learn, whatever our experience be of the power of self, in its sin or its impotence to conquer sin, in its open outbreaks or its hidden power, to see that here is the only cure—at once gently to sink down before God in a humility that confesses its nothingness; in the meekness that bows under and quietly bears the shame we feel: in a patience that waits God's sure deliverance; and a resignation that gives itself entirely to His will, and power, and mercy.[12]

It is in denying self that the fruit of the Spirit comes, and that is far more precious than any kind of self-esteem, self-acceptance, or self-love.

Dobson objects to such worm theology as sinking "down before God in a humility that confesses its nothingness," for he confuses recognizing one's own nothingness and depravity with self hatred and personal disgust. He says:

> Nowhere do I find a commandment that I am to hate myself and live in shame and personal disgust. Unfortunately, I know many Christians who are crushed with feelings of inferiority. Some have been taught this concept of worthlessness by their church.[13]

While groveling about in one's own worthlessness can be just as self-centered as parading about in pride, focusing on personal worthiness is not the way out of self. In the same article, Dobson encourages both a sense of worth (self-esteem) and "esteeming others higher than ourselves." But attempting to combine the commands of Scripture with the ways of the world is like trying to do what is pleasing to God through fleshly means. The whole matter turns on whether one will walk according to the Spirit or after the flesh.

Unconditional Acceptance

Among the stellar emotional needs of humanistic psychology are *unconditional acceptance, unconditional self-regard, unconditional self-acceptance,* and *unconditional love.* The usual meaning of the word *unconditional* is "without conditions or reservations; absolute." The practical extension of the theories of unconditional love is a permissive attitude and a morally nonrestrictive atmosphere. That means no conditions or restrictions in child rearing, counseling, and other human relationships. Since the parent or counselor is to be giving unconditional love, it must be an absolute love, unrestricted by human feelings or failings, since the very meaning of the word is "absolute." But, if there is any absolute when it comes to love, it is that human love is limited. It is **not** what it was originally created to be, even in the best of people and circumstances, except when Jesus Himself is loving in and through a person.

Erich Fromm, who taught the old Greek philosophy of Protagoras, that man is "the measure of all things,"[14] was an early proponent of unconditional love and taught that one must love himself, accept himself, and esteem himself to reach his highest potential. Fromm, Adler, and Maslow considered these "unconditionals" to be basic human needs, essential to a person's sense of well-being. They taught that people need to be loved and accepted unconditionally—without any conditions of performance. Thus their followers teach that parents must love and accept their children unconditionally. Moreover, they encourage all people to love and accept themselves unconditionally.

Adler, Maslow, Rogers and others believed that a human being will find answers to his own dilemmas and naturally blossom into his best self in an atmosphere of unconditional love and acceptance, by which they meant a permissive, unstructured atmosphere. Nevertheless, as much as they would like to think that they themselves loved their clients unconditionally, the truth of the matter is this: **people are not able to love unconditionally**.

Unconditional love is a myth. That is because the human is naturally self-biased and the human heart is so deceitful that one can fool himself into thinking that he is loving unconditionally, when in fact he has all kinds of conditions. For instance, what kind of unconditional love and unconditional positive regard is at work when the client can no longer pay for services and therapy is discontinued? Furthermore, even the most nondirective counselors express approval or disapproval in subtle, if not direct, ways.[15]

The idea of people improving their life in an atmosphere of unconditional love is founded on the premise that people are born good and that their natural inclination to goodness is thwarted by their environment (mainly parents). In such a system, self is the victim of society but finds salvation, freedom, and fulfillment through unconditional self-love and self-acceptance. That is another gospel.

Unconditional love cannot be based on performance or it wouldn't be unconditional. Therefore, it must be based on the intrinsic worth of the person. Paul Brownback, in his book, *The Danger of Self-Love*, explains it this way:

> . . . by unconditional love we are speaking of love on the basis of being rather than doing. One implication of this teaching is the place of grandeur that it gives to the human being. I am lovable just because I am human;

therefore being human, in and of itself, regardless of what I do with my humanness, must have some sort of independent value or worth. It is by itself a sufficient claim to respect and esteem.[16]

Thus, according to these self theories, everyone is born with the **right** to receive unconditional love and unconditional acceptance throughout his entire life, no matter what! While Dobson does not believe in or teach all of the underlying presuppositions of humanistic psychology, he does believe that all people need unconditional love. He says:

I'm convinced the human spirit craves this kind of unconditional love and experiences something akin to "soul hunger" when it cannot be achieved.[17]

Then as an extra bonus, God is brought in as the primary person who gives unconditional love and acceptance. Dobson declares: "God's acceptance is *unconditional*."[18] He is not alone in that conclusion. A host of well-respected Christian leaders describe God's love as unconditional.

Pastors assigned to shepherd God's flocks, should have been alert to the subtleties of deception that would turn a believer's eyes from God to self. But alas, rather than warning the sheep, many of the shepherds have joined the psychologists and embrace their teachings of unconditional love and unconditional acceptance. The basis for their eager embrace is a misunderstanding of the love of God which passes knowledge. They equate unconditional love and acceptance with the fact that God's love is vast, unfathomable, and unmerited. Then they follow that with the idea that if God loves and accepts people unconditionally, they should also love and accept themselves unconditionally. While this may sound like a logical progression, there are some serious problems with the basic assumptions. Therefore, we must address the question: Is God's love unconditional? Are there any conditions that must be met to become a recipient of His love?

Paul prayed that the believers in Ephesus would be able to comprehend the length, width, depth and height of God's love. He desired that they know the love of Christ, which surpasses knowledge, so that they would be filled with the fullness of God (Ephesians 3:16-19). The wide expanse of God's love has been the theme of the Gospel throughout the ages, for to know His love is to know Him. Therefore, any consideration of His love is highly important and must be based on His revelation of Himself rather than on the imagination of men.

Ever since the rise of secular humanism in this country and especially since the establishment of humanistic psychology, the popular, "relevant" term to describe God's love has been *unconditional*. The thrust of this word in humanistic psychology has been both to give and to expect unconditional love from one another with **no strings attached**. While unconditional love and acceptance supposedly promote change and growth, they make no requirements. But God who is love requires change and enables his children to grow in righteousness. He loves his children too much to leave them the way they are.

In humanistic psychology, parents and society are always the culprits. Since humanistic psychologists believe that every person is born with intrinsic worth and innate goodness, they contend that one main reason people experience emotional and behavioral problems is because they have not received unconditional love from their parents. Following that thesis, Christians have come to believe that the best kind of love is unconditional love. It is the highest love secular humanists know. It is touted as a love that makes no demands for performance, good behavior, or the like. It has also been associated with a kind of permissiveness, since it makes no demands and has no conditions, even though the promoters of the unconditional love jargon would say that unconditional love does not have to dispense with discipline.

Because the concept of unconditional love permeates society and because it is often thought of as the highest form of human love, it is natural for a Christian to use this term to describe God. After all, His love is far greater than any human love imaginable. God's love for humanity is so great the "He gave His only begotten Son that whosoever believeth in Him should not perish, but have everlasting life" (John 3:16). Oh, the magnitude of the cost! We cannot even fathom His love even though our very breath depends on it! His love indeed reaches to the heights and depths. But, is God's love truly unconditional?

God's love is available to human beings by grace alone. There is nothing a person can do to earn that love. There is no good work that is either demanded or even possible. Does that make it unconditional? The Scripture declares that "God commendeth his love toward us, in that, while we were yet sinners, Christ died for us" (Romans 5:8). God's provision of salvation and His forgiveness and love cannot be earned. They can only be received by grace through faith. "That whosoever will" is not a work, but it **is** a condition. Otherwise we would end up with universalism (all people saved) rather than salvation by grace received **through** faith.

We must also ask, does God's love apply to the person who has sinned against the Holy Spirit by refusing to receive His grace throughout his lifetime and who is destined for hell? God chooses upon whom He will place His love and the benefits of his love. Did Jesus ever imply that God's love is unconditional? He said to His disciples:

> He that hath my commandments, and keepeth them, he it is that loveth me: and he that loveth me shall be loved of my Father, and I will love him, and will manifest myself to him (John 14:21).

One might argue, however, that the story of the prodigal son proves unconditional love. It indeed illustrates the vastness of God's love, forgiveness and longsuffering. However, the son repented. If he had had a prosperous evil life he may never have repented. While the father would have waited and hoped, he would not have extended his love. After all, he did not go out searching for him to support his folly. Up to a point this seems to indicate unconditional love, and yet, God is not waiting in ignorance, not knowing what those for whom His son died might be doing. He knows, and there comes a time when those who have refused his offer of love and forgiveness die and face the judgment. It is difficult enough to understand God's love without adding the term *unconditional love* which is loaded with secular, humanistic, psychological connotations. The story of the prodigal son teaches grace, forgiveness and mercy, but not unconditional love.

While God loves with a greater love than humans can comprehend, His holiness and justice also must be taken into consideration. Therefore the term *unconditional love* is inadequate for defining God. It does not account for God's reaction to pompous men who devise plans against Him and His anointed. The psalmist goes so far as to say:

> He that sitteth in the heavens shall laugh: the Lord shall have them in derision.
>
> Then shall he speak to them in his wrath, and vex them in his sore displeasure (Psalm 2:4-5).

And what about Lot's wife as she turned to look at the smoldering cities? Or what about Jesus' words to the cities that refused to repent?

> Woe unto thee, Chorazin! woe unto thee, Bethsaida! for if the mighty works, which were done in you, had been done in Tyre and Sidon, they would have repented long ago in sackcloth and ashes. But I say unto you, It shall be more tolerable for Tyre and Sidon at the day of judgment, than for you. And thou, Capernaum, which art exalted unto heaven, shalt be brought down to hell . . . . it shall be more tolerable for the land of Sodom in the day of judgment, than for thee (Matthew 11:21-24).

Does that sound like unconditional love? But perhaps one could say that God's love for the Christian is unconditional since the Christian partakes of His love and grace through faith. Wouldn't it be better to say that the conditions have been met? Jesus met the first condition, to wash away the sin that God hates. The believer meets the second condition by grace through faith. Or, perhaps it would be better to say that God's love extended to a person is conditioned by His plan to give eternal life to those who believe on His Son. The conditions of God's love are resident within Himself.

There is a strong temptation to use vocabulary that is popular in society in order to make Christianity sound relevant. Christians have something far better than what the world offers, but in expressing that good news they confuse people by using words that are already loaded with humanistic connotations and systems of thought. It would be better not to use the expression *unconditional love* when describing God's love. There are plenty of other good words that do not skew His love or character with psychological distortion.

> In this was manifested the love of God toward us, because that God sent His only begotten Son into the world, that we might live through Him.

> Herein is love, not that we loved God, but that He loved us, and sent His Son to be the propitiation for our sins. . . .

> And we have known and believed the love that God hath to us. God is love; and he that dwelleth in love dwelleth in God, and God in him (1 John 4:9, 10, 16).

Forgiving Self

Since secular humanistic psychological theorists do not believe in God, they serve as their own gods and thereby teach people that they must forgive themselves. Now Christians are parroting those teachings. In telling about a family ski incident that happened in 1982, when he took his children to a more challenging slope than they could manage, Dobson says, "Both kids have forgiven me for my foolish decision, but I still haven't forgiven myself."[19]

What kind of a statement is that? Is it biblical? Psychological? Self-condemning? Self-righteous? Does the Bible tell us to forgive ourselves or to withhold forgiveness from ourselves if we really feel bad about what we did? What does the Bible say about forgiving self?

The Bible has a great deal to say about God forgiving us and us forgiving one another, but it says nothing about forgiving ourselves, because forgiving oneself is not the answer to sin. If an unbeliever forgives himself, for instance, he is still in his sin. If a believer forgives himself, he is taking the place of God. If he says, "I know God has forgiven me, but I just can't forgive myself," he is placing his own judgment above God's merciful provision.

Forgiving self comes from the same humanistic, psychological roots as self-love, self-worth, and self-esteem. These are for people whose god is self—not for those whose God is the Lord. The Bible clearly commands us to love the Lord our God, our neighbor as ourselves, our brothers and sisters in the faith, and even our enemies (Deut. 13:3; Matt. 5:44 & 22:37-40; Mark 12:30,31; Luke 6:27 & 10:27; John 15:12). It also tells us to forgive one another, as God has forgiven us (Eph. 4:32; Col. 3:13).

It is sad to see any Christian think it is his option to forgive or not forgive himself and then not to forgive himself even after years have elapsed. But, when one is committed to psychological self-teachings, such as self-love and self-esteem, self-forgiveness seems like a logical necessity, but it is not biblical.

Forgiveness is meant to be an act of love between persons rather that within one's own self. Self-forgiveness is just one more symptom of humanistic self-love, and self-condemnation is just one more symptom of self as god.

Forgiving or not forgiving self is based on pride. Confessing our sin to God and to one another and then receiving forgiveness from God and one another should result in humility and gratitude. Not receiving and believing God's forgiveness, either by not confessing sin or by holding onto a self-righteousness that says, "I can't forgive myself," is prideful and ungrateful. It places one's own evaluation over God's, and when we've been forgiven by others, it says that their forgiveness is not adequate.

Christians have been saved and forgiven on the basis of the sacrificial death of Jesus, who died in our place. Thus, when God forgives His children, it is finished, signed, sealed, and forgotten. "If we confess our sins, he is faithful and just to forgive us our sins, and to cleanse us from all unrighteousness" (1 John 1:9). "As far as the east is from the west, so far hath he removed our transgressions from us" (Psalm 103:12).

Forgiving God?

A logical, but diabolical extension of teaching people to forgive themselves is teaching people to forgive God. This is another intrusion of psychotherapy and its underlying psychologies into Christianity.

Dobson says he is not a theologian, but he prolifically speaks and writes on theological subjects, albeit from a psychological perspective. In his best-selling book *When God Doesn't Make Sense*, which represents a hodgepodge of good and bad theology, Dobson advises his readers to forgive God:

> There is only one cure for the cancer of bitterness. That is to forgive the perceived offender once and for all, with God's help. As strange as it seems, I am suggesting that some of us need to **forgive God** for those heartaches that are charged to His account. You've carried resentment against Him for years. Now it's time to let go of it. (Emphasis added.)

Anticipating a reaction to what he has just said, Dobson continues by saying:

> Please don't misunderstand me at this point. God is in the business of forgiving us, and it almost sounds blasphemous to suggest that the relationship could be reversed.

Dobson concludes by saying:

> He [God] has done no wrong and does not need our approbation. But the source of bitterness must be admitted before it can be cleansed. There is no better way to get rid of it than to **absolve the Lord of whatever we have harbored**, and then ask His forgiveness for our lack of faith. It's called reconciliation, and it is the only way you will ever be entirely free.[20] (Emphasis added.)

The dictionary defines *blasphemy* as "profane or contemptuous speech, writing, or action concerning God." The above writing by Dobson shows at minimum disrespect, if not outright contempt for God. Referring to his idea of forgiving God, Dobson says, ". . . it almost sounds blasphemous." Does it almost sound blasphemous or is it blasphemous?

Can you imagine saying the Lord's Prayer, coming to the words, "forgive us our debts as we forgive our debtors," and including God among those who have sinned against us? What audacity! What a misunderstanding of who God is and what He has done for sinners! We are the sinners for whom Christ died. He, who knew no sin, paid the penalty for our sins. Why would any human being forgive God unless God has sinned? Is it because twentieth-century Christians are so immersed in self that they have lost sight of God? Is it because the psychological reason for forgiving others is to make oneself feel better?

Did Job ever consider the possibility of forgiving God? He attributed the loss of all his children and all his property as from God.

Then Job arose, and rent his mantle, and shaved his head, and fell down upon the ground, and worshipped, and said, Naked came I out of my mother's womb, and naked shall I return thither: the LORD gave, and the LORD hath taken away; blessed be the name of the LORD. In all this Job sinned not, nor charged God foolishly (Job: 1:20-22).

After he was smitten with boils, he wanted to plead his case before God because he knew God was righteous. But, not once did he think he needed to forgive God. The very idea of forgiving God can only be foolishly entertained as a result of having charged God foolishly, and "In all this Job sinned not, nor charged God foolishly."

Forgive God? Who are we to even think such a thought? We are the creatures; He is the creator. He is eternal, from everlasting to everlasting, perfect in holiness. We are none of those things. His ways are perfect; ours are not. His ways are righteous; ours are not. "God is light, and in Him is no darkness at all" (I John 1:5). We are sinners. What does Dobson mean by advising mere, mortal man, a speck in the cosmos, a brief actor in the course of human history, man who hardly represents a jot or tittle compared to his Maker, to forgive the One who created all that is and oversees all that happens?! This type of distorted theology is something for which Dobson should repent.

If we truly know the character of God, would we ever, ever think of such an outrageous idea? If we know God's character and believe His Word, no such thought would ever cross our minds.

There's more here. To justify man forgiving God, Dobson uses a logical fallacy of false analogy. A logic book says:

To recognize the fallacy of false analogy, look for an argument that draws a conclusion about one thing, event, or practice on the basis of its analogy or resemblance to others. The fallacy occurs when the analogy or resemblance is not sufficient to warrant the conclusion, as when,

for example, the resemblance is not relevant to the posses-
sion of the inferred feature or there are relevant dissimi-
larities.[21]

Dobson gives an example of the late Corrie ten Boom forgiving a man who was a prison guard when she was interned in a
prison camp. The story of Corrie ten Boom forgiving this former
concentration camp guard is poignant and powerful, but it is
not a valid parallel to man forgiving God. This was one person
forgiving another person who had sinned against her, which is
what we are commanded to do. This was **not** Corrie ten Boom
forgiving God. It is doubtful she would ever have considered it.
To do so one must have a high view of self and a low view of
God. This is another example of what happens when a person
attempts to incorporate the selfism of psychology with the
Word of God and another example of how using psychology
transmogrifies truth.

6

Dr. Dobson's Theme of Self-Esteem

Dobson's theme of self-esteem runs through all of his work. He often equates low self-esteem with feelings of inadequacy, inferiority, and self-doubt, as well as with lack of self-acceptance and self-worth. According to Dobson, self-esteem is fragile and easily damaged.[1] He says:

> Every age poses its own unique threats to self-esteem. . . . little children typically suffer a severe loss of status during the tender years of childhood. Likewise, most adults are still attempting to cope with the inferiority experienced in earlier times.[2]

Contrary to what Dobson says, research indicates that children are skillful at maintaining strong self-esteem from a very early age. In fact, they seem to be born with it. Even under the most adverse circumstances, children will value themselves and even build positive illusions to protect themselves from feelings of inferiority. After examining the research on self-perception, Dr. Shelley Taylor, a professor of psychology at UCLA, wrote the book *Positive Illusions: Creative Self-Deception and the Healthy Mind*. She says:

Before the exigencies of the world impinge upon the child's self-concept, the child is his or her own hero. With few exceptions, most children think very well of themselves. They believe they are capable at many tasks and abilities, including those they have never tried. They see themselves as popular. Most kindergartners and first-graders say they are at or near the top of the class. They have great expectations for their future success. Moreover, these grandiose assessments are quite unresponsive to negative feedback, at least until approximately age seven.[3]

Though slightly dampened with reality, positive self-regard continues into adulthood. Here are some of the results of Taylor's investigation:

. . . . most adults hold very positive views of themselves. When asked to describe themselves, most people mention many positive qualities and few, if any, negative ones. Even when people acknowledge that they have faults, they tend to downplay those weaknesses as unimportant or dismiss them as inconsequential. . . . Thus, far from being balanced between positive and negative conceptions, the image that most people hold of themselves is heavily weighted in a positive direction.[4]

Then she asks, "Is the positive self-image an illusion or a reality?" She says that both reality and illusion are involved and cites the following examples:

Most people, for example, see themselves as better than others and as above average on most of their qualities. When asked to describe themselves and other people, most people provide more positive descriptions of themselves than they do of friends. . . . Most people even believe that they drive better than others. For example, in one survey, 90 percent of automobile drivers considered themselves to be better than average drivers. . . . Typically, we see ourselves in more flattering terms than we are seen by others. . . most people appear to be very cognizant of their strengths and assets and considerably less aware of their weaknesses and faults.[5] (Emphasis added.)

But while the research seems to indicate that both children and adults tend to esteem themselves more highly than they ought, Dobson believes just the opposite. He fully believes that feelings of inferiority and self-hatred run rampant through society. Here is his emotional appeal to parents to protect their children from the terrible "agony of inferiority":

Thus, if inadequacy and inferiority are so universally prevalent at all ages of life at this time, we must ask ourselves "why?" Why can't our children grow up accepting themselves as they are? Why do so many feel unloved and unlovable? Why are our homes and schools more likely to produce despair and self-hatred than quiet confidence and respect? Why should each child have to bump his head on the same old rock? These questions are of major significance to every parent who would shield his child from the agony of inferiority.[6]

Dobson begins by saying that "inadequacy and inferiority are . . . universally prevalent at all ages of life at this time." He evidently subscribes to Adler's theories of the universality of inferiority feelings, for this is Dobson's diagnosis of society and the church. Nevertheless, such a statement is too general. Inadequate at what? Inferior to what or whom? And if the problem is inferiority, the answer must be superiority, that is, to be better than others.

The human condition is such that each person has certain capabilities and limitations. But if a person's focus is on self and what self wants, self will be discontent unless it feels as good as or better than the next person. On the other hand, if the focus is on Christ, a person will find his adequacy in Him. Feelings of inferiority and superiority are self-focused, but humility is God-focused and God-honoring. Therefore the problem to be dealt with here is sin and pride.

Dobson's entire statement treats people as victims rather than sinners. Most psychological systems of understanding humanity put people in the role of victim. They are victims of circumstances, past and present. Or, victims of internal drives or so-called unconscious motivations. Or, they have been victimized by people who have not treated them in ways they "deserve" to be treated. But, the Bible declares that people are sinners and Jesus came to save them from their own sin.

Man is not born perfect and good, but rather in the condition of sin with a proclivity to sinning. He is born into the kingdom of darkness and in that kingdom he both sins and is sinned against. Although he is sometimes a victim of the sins of others, he finds his way out of the kingdom of darkness through recognizing by God's grace that he is a sinner separated from God. Therefore, the Bible does not emphasize the victim aspects of mankind, but rather reveals the condition of sin. Confessing one's own sinfulness is an integral part of salvation and confessing one's own sinful acts is an essential ongoing activity of sanctification. And all of that is through the conviction of the Holy Spirit and the grace of God.

After diagnosing inadequacy and inferiority as "universally prevalent," Dobson asks, "Why can't our children grow up accepting themselves as they are?" Self-acceptance is an extremely important concept of humanistic psychology, but it is not found anywhere in the Bible. The Bible stresses being content with what we have, whether it be physical appearance, ability, inability, success or lack of success, popularity or lack of friends, material possessions or even near poverty. It may be that those who seem to exhibit lack of self-acceptance are actually covetous, wanting what they don't have to the point of allowing covetousness to rule their heart and motivate their behavior.

God makes the provision in Hebrews 13:5:

Let your conversation be without covetousness; and be content with such things as ye have: for He hath said, I will never leave thee nor forsake thee.

This means that Christians are not to be motivated by lust for what we lack. They are to be content with what they have, because Jesus is always with them. The promise that so many Christians recite, "I will never leave thee nor forsake thee," is connected to being satisfied with God's provisions, no matter how scant they may appear, because the sovereign God of the universe has promised always to be with His children. He will enable believers to do His will and He will sustain them with His grace.

The difference between self-acceptance and being content with what we have may seem subtle, because there are areas of similarity. For instance one can say that a child who is dissatisfied with his physical appearance is being covetous for what he does not have **or** that he is not accepting himself. Either way he may be miserable. If he is taught to be content with what he has because of Jesus' promise to always be with him, he may learn to walk in the Spirit. If, on the other hand, he is taught to esteem and accept himself, he will learn to walk in the flesh. From the viewpoint of an outside observer there may not seem to be much difference, but from God's perspective the difference is tremendous.

Parents who do not know God will want to use effective means of teaching their children to walk after the flesh and according to the ways of the world. And we can understand why secular schools work to build self-acceptance in the children. But it is anathema for Christian leaders to encourage parents to rear children according to the ways of the world— the ways of self—instead of the ways of the Lord.

But, you may say, when Christians use the term *self-acceptance* they mean being content with physical appearance, abilities, etc. If that is what is meant, then that is what should be said. Careful choice of words is essential because the term *self-acceptance* carries far more baggage than simply being content with what God has given. Self-acceptance implies acceptance of oneself just the way one is, without any need to change behavior or attitude unless the self wants to change. It implies a judgment of I am good just the way I am; I don't need to change; I'm okay now.

Self-acceptance is a self-focusing activity drawing the eyes and heart away from God's presence, provisions, will, and even His love. A solid wall of self-acceptance can serve as a barrier to the conviction of the Holy Spirit. It more resembles a heart of stone than one which is sensitive to the presence of the Holy Spirit. In *An Exposition of the Sermon on the Mount*, A. W. Pink says, "Man must be humbled into the dust before he will, as a beggar, betake himself to the Redeemer," and that one must "be emptied of self-righteousness, self-esteem, and self-sufficiency."[7]

Next Dobson asks, "Why do so many feel unloved and unlovable?" Is the answer more self-esteem or is it the love of God? The most important criteria for love in the family is the centrality of Jesus Christ, but Dobson barely touches on this essential truth in *Hide or Seek*. Godly ways are passed on from generation to generation through words and actions, but so are sinful ways. Therefore, the parents' own walk with the Lord will have consequences for their children and grandchildren for either good or ill.

The Bible addresses this issue:

> And the LORD passed by before him [Moses] and proclaimed, The LORD , The LORD God, merciful and gracious, long-suffering, abundant in goodness and truth, Keeping mercy for thousands, forgiving iniquity and transgression and sin, and that will by no means clear the guilty; visiting the iniquity of the fathers upon the children, and upon the children's children, unto the third and to the fourth generation (Exodus 34:6-7).

> But the mercy of the LORD is from everlasting to everlasting upon them that fear Him, and His righteousness unto

children's children; to such as keep his covenant, and to those that remember his commandments to do them (Psalm 103:17-18).

Much suffering can come into the lives of children whose parents do not love and obey God. However, Jesus can break the power of sin in people's lives so that they can walk in new life with Him, even if their parents did not love the Lord or walk according to His ways.

The influence of each generation upon another is greater than any superimposed teaching, unless they are teachings that come from the Bible and are energized by the Holy Spirit. Expressing love and administering discipline in effective ways are definitely taught in the Bible. But beyond that, they are lived through the crucified life, that is, through the indwelling life of Jesus rather than by the ways of the self.

Dobson's next question is: "Why are our homes and schools more likely to produce despair and self-hatred than quiet confidence and respect?" Our schools are mainly secular and many Christians schools have a secular mind-set. Furthermore, as much as we would like to deny it, most Christians also have a secular mind-set filled with psychological notions. Without the Lord there is despair at some point along the way. The centrality of Jesus Christ in a person's life is the answer, not higher self-esteem.

Dobson's next question is: "Why should each child have to bump his head on the same old rock?" But isn't the "same old rock" all of what is implied in our fallenness and living in a fallen world which is in rebellion against God? And isn't the answer found only in Jesus? As much as parents would like to protect their children from all of the bumps and bruises of life, they can't. Therefore, the best they can do for them is to teach them the ways of God through what they say and do.

When Dobson refers to the "agony of inferiority" he is not speaking of actual inferiority, but rather the experience and feelings of inferiority or low-self esteem. He believes that such feelings are excruciating. He further contends that *"the* most dominant force" which motivates people is avoidance of that pain. Dobson says:

> You see, damage to the ego (loss of self-worth) actually equals or exceeds the pain of physical discomfort in intensity. . . . So painful is its effect that our entire emotional apparatus is designed to protect us from its oppression. *In other words, a sizable proportion of all human activity is devoted to the task of shielding us from the inner pain of inferiority.* I believe this to be the most dominant force in life, even exceeding the power of sex and its influence.[8] (Emphasis his.)

That statement demonstrates how fully Dobson subscribes to Adler's and Maslow's theories of motivation. However, in their book *Psychology's Sanction for Selfishness*, Michael and Lise Wallach look at those theories of motivation and say:

> Our analysis suggests that the roots of psychology's ubiquitous sanction for selfishness lie in fundamental assumptions about motivation that almost all psychologists have come to take for granted. We attempt to demonstrate that these assumptions constitute holdovers from a time when they possessed a scientific plausibility that they now lack. The directions taken by psychological theorizing that serve to support and encourage selfishness do not, we find, seem justified in the light of current knowledge and evidence. Counter to the thrust of most thinking about motivation, a different picture may be emerging, suggesting that we can be genuinely motivated by ends outside of ourselves. . . .[9]

Dobson is among the "almost all psychologists" who "have come to take for granted" those "fundamental assumptions about motivation." Therefore, Dobson blames low self-esteem for causing all kinds of problems and touts high self-esteem as an absolute necessity for survival. Thus raising children's self-esteem appears to be the motive behind all of his advice in *Hide or Seek*.

While some of Dobson's strategies and suggestions line up with biblical principles of child rearing, the motives and goals differ. While the Bible tells us to love, value and esteem our children, it does not tell us to raise their self-esteem. We are to love, value, esteem, and instruct our children so that they will grow up in the nurture and admonition of the Lord, so that they might become His loving children and His obedient servants. The self-esteem motive and goal are man-centered, while the biblical motive and goal are Christ-centered.

Dobson's "Strategies for Self-Esteem"

Most of the self-esteem literature, both in the world and in the church, give three general ways that a person develops self-esteem. They are: through personal achievement, from working on one's own subjective view of self, and from the response of others to oneself. Like his humanistic counterparts, Dobson gives methods for boosting self-esteem. In *Hide or Seek*, which is based on the premise that self-esteem is a crucial need of every person, he has a section entitled "Strategies for Self-Esteem," in which he suggests "ways to teach a child of his genuine significance."[10] In this section he stresses the method of developing self-esteem through achievement. He does this in an attempt to counteract negative responses from others which may be based on superficial, damaging evaluations of such things as beauty or intelligence.

Dobson stresses achievement as the road to self-esteem and suggests ways for parents to help their children compensate. On the surface, such a strategy sounds great. But what might parents be communicating? Would children then learn that they can feel good about themselves if they are better than others? And should Christians base human worth on achievement and success according to the world's standards? If parents thus teach their children that they can gain value through being able to swim better than somebody else, for instance, what about the child who dearly wants to be able to swim well but can't even make the swim team? Will he somehow be devalued as well by a society with the wrong values?

Compensation is the attempt to make up for a deficiency. A person may thus compensate for his inabilities in one area by achieving in another area. Dobson even attributes power for success to what he calls "the need to compensate." He says:

> The power behind these and other kinds of success almost invariably springs from the need for self-worth— the need to prove something about one's adequacy—the need to *compensate!*[11] (Emphasis his.)

He declares: "*Succinctly stated, compensation is your child's best weapon against inferiority.*"[12] (Emphasis his.) However, the very idea of compensation implies that we'll feel better about ourselves if we are in some way better than others. Rather than emphasizing biblical standards and behavior, compensation emphasizes comparing ourselves with each other, which the Bible calls unwise (2 Corinthians 10:12). Furthermore, such compensation may lead to competitiveness which nurtures pride rather than love for others.

Adler believed that inferiority feelings motivate nearly all behavior. He taught that people strive for superiority in order to overcome feelings of inferiority. Dobson continues the tradition by encouraging compensation to overcome inferiority and low self-esteem.[13]

In a letter written to Dobson, Dave Hunt questioned the use of compensation to build self-esteem:

> I do not deny that there are people who feel worthless and incapable of doing anything. However, I do deny that attempting to build up their self-esteem is the right solution—it certainly is not the Biblical one. They need to turn from themselves to the Lord. Rather than compensating (as you advocate) by developing some skill that

will gain the admiration of their peers, they need to seek God's approval and learn to stand true to Him in spite of opposition from others. The Bible is full of people who were nobodies in their own eyes and in the eyes of others; who were hated and cast out by friends and family and who found their joy and confidence not in self-esteem or self-worth but in turning from themselves to trust and rejoice in the Lord.[14]

Along with his humanistic colleagues, Dobson also stresses that one must work on one's own subjective self-evaluation for worth. In *Hide or Seek*, Dobson boldly asserts:

Don't you see that **your personal worth is not really dependent on the opinions of others** and the temporal, fluctuating values they represent? The sooner you can accept the transcending worth of your humanness, the sooner you can come to terms with yourself.[15] (Emphasis added.)

However, he contradicts himself and limits the way to self-esteem in his book *What Wives Wish Their Husbands Knew About Women*. There he declares:

Feelings of self-worth and acceptance, which provide the cornerstone of a healthy personality, can be obtained from only *one* source. . . . Self-esteem is **only** generated by what we see reflected about ourselves in the eyes of other people. It is only when others respect us that we respect ourselves. It is only when others love us that we love ourselves. It is only when others find us pleasant and desirable and worthy that we come to terms with our own egos.[16] (Italic emphasis his; bold emphasis added.)

In response to this statement, Dr. Robert Smith says:

In John 12:43 is Christ's criticism of people who loved the praise of men more than the praise of God. Self-esteem philosophy teaches us that we must have the praise of men before we can function properly. It is regrettable that believers accept this unbiblical, even anti-biblical philosophy and teach it as a necessity for other believers.[17]

In stressing how dependent self-esteem is on the response of others, Dobson seems to negate his other suggestions for building self esteem. Besides the obvious contradiction, it is interesting to note how the new morality of self-love has changed the picture. It used to be that children learned to love others by being loved, to respect others by being respected, to esteem others by being esteemed, and to treat others with kindness by being treated that way. Before this psychological era, the emphasis was on others rather than on self. And the emphasis in the Bible is on loving, respecting, and esteeming God and others since the Bible says that we already do love ourselves (Ephesians 5:29).

Adolescents and Self-Esteem

One of Dobson's primary purposes of writing *Preparing for Adolescence* was to help teenagers deal with feelings of self-doubt, inferiority, and low self-esteem. He declares that the adolescent years are "the most stressful and threatening time of life" with "scary physical changes," "sexual anxieties," "self-doubt and feelings of inferiority," which at times seem "unbearable."[18] His first chapter is "The Secret of Self-Esteem." Dobson dramatically describes the "Agony of Inferiority" or the "feeling of hopelessness that we call 'inferiority.'" He says:

It's that awful awareness that nobody likes you, that you're not as good as other people, that you're a failure, a loser, a personal disaster; that you're ugly, or unintelligent, or don't have as much ability as someone else. It's that depressing feeling of worthlessness.[19]

Dobson bemoans, "What a shame that most teenagers decide they are without much human worth when they're between thirteen and fifteen years of age."[20] (Emphasis his.) He likens it to a "dark hole in the roadway to adulthood that captures so many young people."[21] He says:

> We *all* have human worth, yet so many young people conclude that they're somehow different—that they're truly inferior—that they lack the necessary ingredients for dignity and worth.[22] (Emphasis his.)

In order to illustrate how terrible teenagers feel, Dobson describes the feelings of two teenagers who have no friends. Then he poses these questions, "Why do so many teenagers feel inferior? Why can't American young people grow up liking themselves?"[23] Then he describes "the three things that teenagers feel they *must* have in order to feel good about themselves."[24] (Emphasis his.) The first is physical attractiveness and he claims that eighty percent of the teenagers are dissatisfied with their appearance. Then he lists intelligence as second and money as third.

Here again, in *Preparing for Adolescence* Dobson offers a number of suggestions to deal with inferiority feelings, one of which is compensation, as in *Hide or Seek*. He also suggests making friends. The purpose for friendship here seems to be that *"nothing helps your self-confidence more than genuine friends."*[25] (Emphasis his.) Why? Because, he reasons, "If you know that other people like you it's much easier to accept yourself."[26] Yet, this does not seem to be a very dependable source for building self-confidence or self-esteem since Dobson declares in *The Strong-Willed Child*: "An adolescent's worth as a human being hangs precariously on peer group acceptance, which is notoriously fickle."[27] Furthermore, the point of friendship seems to be selfish to begin with if it is to build one's own self-esteem.

One of the causes that Dobson attributes to an adolescent's low self-esteem actually reveals a high level of self-esteem, self-regard, and self-justification. Dobson says:

> The self-esteem of an early adolescent is also assaulted in the Western culture by his youthful status. All of the highly advertised adult privileges and vices are forbidden to him because he is "too young." He can't drive or marry or enlist or drink or smoke or work or leave home. And his sexual desires are denied gratification at a time when they scream for release. The only thing he is permitted to do, it seems, is stay in school and read his dreary textbooks. This is an overstatement, of course, but it is expressed from the viewpoint of the young man or woman who feels disenfranchised and insulted by society. Much of the anger of today's youth is generated by their perception of this "injustice."28

Such expectations—to have adult privileges—and such anger at this "injustice" indicates high self-esteem and high self-worth. The teenager described here seems to think he is worthy of more than what he is getting—certainly worthy of more than school and "dreary textbooks." Is this low-self-esteem or is it a covetous attitude of not being content and grateful for what one already has? The problem seems to be that the culture does not regard the teenager as highly as he seems to regard himself, according to Dobson's description on assaulted self-esteem.

To prove a point, such as a universal occurrence of low self-esteem making adolescents vulnerable to peer pressure, Dobson uses interviews or group discussion. What he does not say is that in such an arrangement the discussion leader can usually draw out the kind of material he's looking for. The same thing happens in therapy. For instance, a Freudian analyst may encourage the client to talk about dreams. Pretty soon, there are all kinds of dreams and much material that will fit perfectly with dream theory. Or, a person in Jungian analysis will soon be giving all kinds of evidence of archetypes. With the right kinds of leading questions, a person can find what he's looking for.

In *Preparing for Adolescence*, Dobson includes his discussion/interview with a group of teenagers to illustrate his belief in the universality of feelings of inferiority, low self-esteem and lack of self-acceptance. Naturally every participant joins in and has something to say to support Dobson's assumption that teens are suffering enormously from those crippling psychological conditions. Each participant has a few incidents to relate which seem to support Dobson's ideas that all teens live under horrible conditions which are almost impossible to overcome unless their self-esteem is raised. Again, self-esteem becomes the antidote to nearly everything, including peer pressure.[29]

Such a discussion can actually stimulate participants to say what the leader wants to have said. Among the teenagers participating in the interview was a boy who is called Greg in the text. Early in his interview of Greg, Dobson asks how people get started taking drugs. Greg says:

> Well, I started taking drugs because I was inquisitive, and bored, and because it was an easy way of being entertained.[30]

Later Dobson gets into ideas of inferiority and drug abuse and says:

> Greg, I would like you to comment on the role which inferiority plays in drug abuse, which we were discussing earlier. **As you know, it is my belief that the person who feels inferior—the person who doesn't like himself—sometimes takes drugs to escape. . . . Did feelings of inferiority play a role in your own experience?**[31]

Greg answers: "Absolutely. Inferiority played the most significant role in my case."[32] But inferiority was not the reason he gave earlier. Before Dobson convinced him of low self-esteem as the reason for such things, Greg had said:

> Well, I started taking drugs because I was inquisitive, and bored, and because it was an easy way of being entertained.[33]

Just as Dobson fed Greg the low self-esteem explanation for why he took drugs, self-esteemers throughout the nation are convincing people that their problems are due to inferiority and low self-esteem.

Again, research gives a different picture. In his book *The Inflated Self*, David Myers says that "it appears that high school students are not racked with inferiority feelings." He cites the findings from the College Board taken by large numbers of high school seniors and reports:

> In "leadership ability," 70% rated themselves above average, two percent as below average. Sixty percent viewed themselves as better than average in "athletic ability," only 6% as below average. In "ability to get along with other," *zero* percent of 829,000 students who responded rated themselves below average, 60% rated themselves in the top 10%, and 25% saw themselves among the top 1%.

Myers concludes: "Consciously, at least, a 'superiority complex' predominates over the inferiority complex."[34] Why does Dobson ignore such data? We provide even more evidence of this in a later chapter.

Is the real problem low self-esteem, or have people been taught to define their disappointments and difficulties that way? Some people are actually relieved when they are told that their problem is low self-esteem. Here is an easy explanation for what's wrong and it requires no more than to love, esteem, cater to, and coddle the self. It also gives a convenient excuse for bad behavior. In fact, the concept of low self-esteem can give a person a handy scapegoat and an excuse for further sin.

Dobson contends that peer pressure **causes** certain behavior. This separates behavior from personal choice. He says:

> And that [peer] pressure can cause you to behave in ways that you know are harmful. I believe, for example that most of the drug abuse in our country occurs because of the enormous pressure that Gaylene [discussion group member] described.[35]

In relating peer pressure to feelings of inferiority during the teenage years, Dobson reasons that young people are more likely to conform out of fear of ridicule and rejection if they have low self-esteem. And, then of course, conformity leads to taking drugs, etc.[36] As we demonstrate later, this assumption on Dobson's part is false.

In an attempt to raise their self-esteem, Dobson assures teenagers that God loves them, but he neglects to teach them the fear of the Lord. Only fear of the Lord can replace fear of men. Those who fear men have an inadequate fear of the Lord. Those who fear the Lord understand who God is. Jesus said:

> And fear not them which kill the body, but are not able to kill the soul; but rather fear him which is able to destroy both soul and body in hell (Matthew 10:28).

Rather than writing a book to teenagers stressing that fear of the Lord is the beginning of wisdom, Dobson teaches that the way to overcome fear of rejection is to have high self-esteem. What works for the world works for Dobson's system. The Lord is brought in primarily as an assurance for personal worth.

And, indeed, Jesus speaks of worth in this same passage. He speaks of the Father's loving care by saying that "the very hairs of your head are all numbered." Then he says, "Fear ye not therefore, ye are of more value than many sparrows" (Matt: 10:30-31). However, Jesus is not saying those words to just anybody. He is saying them to His disciples while He was commissioning them to go to the cities to preach that the Kingdom was at hand. Yes, those who follow and serve God do not have to fear men, because God has chosen to place His love upon them and to protect them from the second death.

Jesus words are not to build self-esteem, but rather to give his disciples courage to follow Him even to the point of death. His words are **not** to raise a person from feelings of inferiority to superiority or self-confidence. Jesus wants to get our eyes off ourselves and onto Him. Rather than looking at our own inadequacies, He calls us to gaze upon His love and trust Him to enable us to please God.

Women and Self-Esteem

Not only does Dobson believe that children and teenagers are fraught with the blight of inferiority and low self-esteem; he is convinced that this is the plight of women as well. He declares: "Even that word 'housewife' has come to symbolize unfulfillment, inferiority, and insignificance."[37] He contends that "feelings of inadequacy, lack of confidence, and certainty of worthlessness have become a way of life, or too often, a way of despair for millions of American women."[38]

Dobson dramatically describes a woman's low self-esteem this way:

> It is sitting alone in a house during the quiet afternoon hours, wondering why the phone doesn't ring. . . wondering why you have no "real" friends. It is longing for someone to talk to, soul to soul, but knowing there is no such person worthy of your trust. . . . It is wondering why other people have so much more talent and ability than you do. It is feeling incredibly ugly and sexually unattractive. It is admitting that you have become a failure as a wife and mother. It is disliking everything about yourself and wishing, constantly wishing, you could be someone

else. It is feeling unloved and unlovable and lonely and sad. It is lying in bed after the family is asleep, pondering the vast emptiness inside and longing for unconditional love. It is intense self-pity. It is reaching up in the darkness to remove a tear from the corner of your eye. *It is depression!*[39] (Emphasis his.)

Note that at the end of his description of low self-esteem, Dobson says, "*It is depression!*" He has thus said that low self-esteem and depression are the same thing. And while that kind of thinking can be depressing, one needs to ask if that is a description of low self-esteem or self pity? To call this low self-esteem makes the woman a victim, but to admit that it is the self-centered activity of feeling sorry for oneself makes the woman a sinner. And Jesus came to redeem and forgive sinners and to restore them to fellowship with God so that the promise of His presence, "I will never leave thee nor forsake thee," would enable them to be content (Hebrews 13:5).

Could what poses as low-self-esteem actually be wounded pride, a burdened conscience, and dissatisfaction with circumstances? As one man asked us: "Have you considered the possibility that so-called low self-esteem is the product of the tension between what we or others think about ourselves and what our pride will not accept?"[40] In a letter to Dobson, author T. A. McMahon says:

> I would encourage you to go back over the examples you consider as symptoms of "low self-esteem." It seems it's not self they're having problems with but rather *circumstances*. They are usually upset or depressed, not because they have a low opinion of themselves, but rather the circumstances may be forcing them to reduce their high or even "healthy" opinion of themselves. . . . If one truly had a low opinion of himself it would make more sense if he weren't at all affected by embarrassing or demeaning circumstances.[41] (Emphasis his.)

In Dobson's description of low self-esteem nearly every aspect is a sinful attitude and/or a self-focus. Thus "sin" is replaced with "low self-esteem." If these attitudes are sin, the remedy is repentance and development of new attitudes and actions through the Word of God and the work of the Holy Spirit. But if one calls sin "low self-esteem," the obvious remedy applied is to raise the self-esteem. If one repents and is renewed in his mind, there is true biblical remedy. But if the remedy is raising self-esteem, the results may indeed be more sin, even though that sin may be hidden in the heart with self on the throne.

Dobson also relates self-esteem to women's hormones. He says, "Since self-esteem is apparently related to estrogen, for example, a woman's feelings of inferiority are evident both pre-menstrually and during menopause."[42] An endocrinologist on the faculty of a medical school responded to Dobson's views about estrogens as being "simplistic."[43] It would be just as plausible and simplistic to say that feeling sorry for oneself is related to estrogen. Nevertheless from Dobson's description of low self-esteem, he seems to attribute any negative feelings to low self-esteem.

Medical doctor Robert D. Smith takes issue with Dobson's medical advice in *What Wives Wish their Husbands Knew about Women*. He says:

> Dr. Dobson has formulated a medical philosophy without adequate medical knowledge and has based it upon testimonial evidence. He states that, "Self-esteem is directly related to estrogen levels." (151) There is no proof that such a thing exists or that lack of estrogen produces depression, as he so vigorously states. It is interesting to read his attitude stated on page 150. "My experience with this woman and similar patients has given me an intolerance for physicians who don't believe in hormonal therapy even though it is so obviously needed."[44]

Then Smith refers to a note which Dobson added to the end of this section in his revised edition, which says in very fine print:

> Since this book was first published in 1975, several clinical researchers have observed an apparent link between estrogen therapy and cancer of the uterus. However, this and other potential side effects of hormone replacement therapy remain controversial issues in medical circles and are being debated vigorously from both points of view. Further investigations are currently in progress. It is advised that women with menopausal symptoms seek and accept the counsel of their physicians.[45]

Smith remarks:

> It is interesting how he describes an intolerance [for physicians] in his major portion, but in the footnote decides that it is better that they [the women] seek the counsel of a physician.[46]

Dobson says that he emphasizes the impact of low self-esteem on women because "the 'disease' of inferiority has reached epidemic proportions among females, particularly, at this time in our history."[47] Then he goes on to tell us the reason: "Their traditional responsibilities have become matters of disrespect and ridicule."[48]

Women have been the target for all kinds of "mental diseases" from Freud onward. We can all thank Freud for putting much of the blame for neurosis and psychosis on mothers. Furthermore, women are regularly diagnosed with such labels as "masochism," "depression," and "low self-esteem." Generally male psychologists and psychiatrists are the ones who have perpetrated this on women. (No wonder they have "low self-esteem"!)

One of Dobson's primary objectives of writing *What Wives Wish Their Husbands Knew about Women* was to "Discuss the

common sources of depression in women, and their solutions."[49] He says:

> Perhaps the most inescapable conclusion I have drawn
> from psychological counseling of women concerns the
> commonness of depression and emotional apathy as a
> recurring fact of life. The majority of adult females seem
> to experience these times of despair, discouragement,
> disinterest, distress, despondency, and disenchantment
> with circumstances as they are.[50]

Dobson lists "Fatigue and Time Pressure" as the second
greatest cause of depression. Of course in Dobson's scheme
that, too, is linked with self-esteem, since being over-extended
may lead to failure in certain areas with self-esteem being
further damaged.[51]

Dobson devised a short check list called "Sources of Depression among Women." Because of the nature of the check list
there was no indication as to how depressed these women actually were. It just asked the women to rank reasons for their
depression. And, of course the top ranking reason was "Low
self-esteem." He says he was surprised because most of the
women who filled out the questionnaire appeared to be
"healthy, happily married, attractive young women who seemingly had everything to live for."[52] One wonders if the reason
they checked low self-esteem might be because they have
learned to equate general feelings of discontent with low self-
esteem. Or, perhaps it demonstrates the amount of personal
dissatisfaction that comes from thinking about oneself too
much. However, the conclusion which Dobson draws from his
questionnaire is that "inferiority and inadequacy have become
constant companions of many, perhaps most, American women
today."[53]

According to Dobson, low-self esteem not only causes
depression. He says, "Lack of self-esteem produces more symptoms of psychiatric disorders than any other factor yet identified."[54] Furthermore, he contends that low self-esteem leads to

denial of reality which leads to both alcoholism and psychotic experience.[55] Since he believes that women are suffering from an epidemic of low self-esteem, Dobson valiantly declares:

> If I could write a prescription for the women of the world, it would provide each one of them with a healthy dose of self-esteem and personal worth (taken three times a day until the symptoms disappear). I have no doubt that this is their greatest need.[56]

Is self-esteem a woman's greatest need? Then why is it absent from the Bible? Why didn't Jesus meet this greatest need of women? Why didn't Jesus address self-esteem with the woman at the well? Why didn't he admonish Martha for having low self esteem? Dobson doesn't seem to notice this because of his commitment to need psychology.

Self-esteem teachings only enable a person to move from a miserable form of self-centeredness (called low self-esteem, poor self-image, so-called self-hatred) to a more self-pleasing form of self-centeredness with high self-esteem, self-love, self-worth, and self-acceptance. And, while people may tend to cope with feelings of inferiority through becoming superior (through achievement) or through positive illusions (self-deception), these are activities of the flesh, not of the Spirit. This is the way of the world and the way of pride, as deceptively hidden as it may be. This is about all the world has to offer. Because it appeals to the fleshly self, there are Christians who are seeking the "best" that the world seems to offer.

While the world touts the benefits of self-esteem, the Bible clearly says, "The just shall live by faith," and that means faith in God, not faith in self (Romans 1:17). Following the self-esteem bandwagon leads to being conformed to this world rather than being "transformed by the renewing of your mind, that ye may prove what is that good, and acceptable, and perfect, will of God" (Romans 12:2).

7

The California Task Force on Self-Esteem

If there is one thing the world and many in the church have in common these days, it's the psychology of self-esteem. Although they may disagree about some of the nuances of self-esteem, self-worth, and self-acceptance, and even on some of the finer points of definition, they have joined forces against the formidable enemy, low self-esteem. Many in both the church and the world would agree with Dobson's ominous assessment:

> In fact, low self-esteem is a threat to the entire human family, affecting children, adolescents, the elderly, all socioeconomic levels of society, and each race and ethnic culture.[1]

Dobson is quite compatible with the self-esteem movement nationally, as well as in California. He is, of course, the first name that comes up when the subject of self-esteem surfaces in the church. And there is an unmistakable harmony between the secular self-esteem movement and the self-esteem espoused by Dobson.

The California legislature passed a bill creating the California Task Force to Promote Self-Esteem and Personal and Social Responsibility. The legislature funded the bill with $245,000 a year for three years, for a total of $735,000. The twofold title of the Task Force is an assumption and may, in fact, be a contradiction. No one has ever demonstrated that promoting self-esteem is in any way related to personal and social responsibility. Nor has anyone ever proved that all those who exhibit personal and social responsibility have high self-esteem. No doubt the "personal and social responsibility" had to be tacked on to promoting self-esteem or the bill would probably never have been passed. Self-esteem and social and personal responsibility may actually be negatively rather than positively related.

The Mission Statement of the Task Force states:

> Seek to determine whether self-esteem, and personal and social responsibility are the keys to unlocking the secrets of healthy human development so that we can get to the roots of and develop effective solutions for major social problems and to develop and provide for every Californian the latest knowledge and practices regarding the significance of self-esteem, and personal and social responsibility.[2]

The Task Force believes that esteeming oneself and growing in self-esteem will reduce "dramatically the epidemic levels of social problems we currently face."[3] Such statements made by the Task Force often sound very much like what Dobson says. For instance, in his book *Hide or Seek* he says:

> The matter of personal worth is not only the concern of those who lack it. In a real sense, the health of an entire society depends on the ease with which its individual members can gain personal acceptance. *Thus, whenever the keys to self-esteem are seemingly out of reach for a*

large percentage of the people, as in twentieth-century America, then widespread "mental illness," neuroticism, hatred, alcoholism, drug abuse, violence, and social disorder will certainly occur.[4] (Emphasis his.)

As further evidence of the identification between Dobson's self-esteem position and the Task Force is the fact that Dobson was featured in their *Esteem* publication. Considering how few people were featured over the three year period and the fact that Dobson was one of them speaks volumes. In addition, Dobson was listed in the Task Force publication *Self-Esteem Curricular Resources, Books and Other Resources.* We called the Task Force office and asked if Dobson objected to being featured in the *Esteem* publication or listed in the resource publication and we were told "no." In addition, his book *Hide or Seek* is on their recommended reading list. *Hide or Seek* and *Dare to Discipline* fit so well with the secular mind-set that even the popular radio psychologist Dr. Toni Grant recommended them on her show.[5]

One additional interesting relationship between the Task Force and Dobson is that Dr. Kenneth Ogden, a member of the Task Force, has been involved at the Focus on the Family ministries. He directed a Counseling Enrichment Program sponsored by Focus on the Family.[6]

Dobson's view of self-esteem and its effect on the individual and society is quite compatible with that of the Task Force. However, temporally ignoring whether self-esteem teachings *a la* Task Force or Dobson are biblical, let us see what the relationship is between self-esteem and major social problems. Is there a positive relationship between high or low self-esteem and personal and social responsibility?

Does Low Self-Esteem Cause Problem Behavior?

In order to investigate this relationship the state Task Force hired eight professors from the University of California to look at the research on self-esteem as it relates to the six following areas:

1. Crime, violence and recidivism.
2. Alcohol and drug abuse.
3. Welfare dependency.
4. Teenage pregnancy.
5. Child and spousal abuse.
6. Children failing to learn in school.

Seven of the professors researched the above areas and the eighth professor summarized the results. The results were then published in a book titled *The Social Importance of Self-Esteem*.[7] In the Second Annual Progress Report of the Task Force on self-esteem, The Executive Summary states:

> The statute creating the Task Force posed this as a basic question: What is the extent of the correlation between low self-esteem and six major social concerns (crime and violence, drug and alcohol abuse, teen pregnancy, child and spousal abuse, chronic welfare dependency, and the failure to achieve in school)? Based on their first-hand experiences most therapists, counselors, teachers, and other social service professionals have long been certain of a direct link between low self-esteem and these personal and social ills, but there had not previously existed any recognized academic evidence of this connection. Now that evidence is in hand.[8]

Has the relationship been established between self-esteem and social problems? Dr. Neil Smelser, the professor who summarized the research presented in *The Social Importance of Self-Esteem*, says:

> The research reviewed in the following chapters has been carried out primarily with small ad hoc samples generated by researchers who have pulled together the sample

from groups that were available to them through some personal or institutional contact. Small samples yield relations that cannot be regarded as statistically significant; when uncovered, these relations cannot permit causal inferences; and, above all, small samples do not permit the holding constant of other variables suspected of affecting the relationships between self-esteem and some outcomes.[9]

Smelser admits:

One of the disappointing aspects of every chapter in this volume. . . is how low the associations between self-esteem and its consequences are in research to date.[10]

Smelser also says:

The authors who have assessed the state-of-the-art knowledge of factors important in the genesis of many social problems have been unable to uncover many causally valid findings relating to that genesis—and they have therefore been correspondingly unable to come up with systematic statements relating to cure or prevention.[11]

David L. Kirk, syndicated writer for the *San Francisco Examiner*, says it more bluntly:

The Social Importance of Self-Esteem summarizes all the research on the subject in the stultifyingly boring prose of wannabe scientists. Save yourself the 40 bucks the book costs and head straight for the conclusion: There is precious little evidence that self-esteem is the cause of our social ills.[12]

Kirk further says:

Those social scientists looked hard . . . but they could detect essentially **no cause-and-effect link between self-esteem and problematic behavior, whether it's teen pregnancy, drug use or child abuse.**[13] (Emphasis added.)

The research presented in that book is replete with statistical and methodological problems. Anyone who uses the book and its findings to support self-esteem as the cause or cure for the "epidemic level of social problems" listed above is grossly distorting the research.

John Vasconcellos, the California Assemblyman who authored the self-esteem legislation, says that self-esteem "most likely appears to be the social vaccine that inoculates us to lead lives apart from drugs and violence."[14] However, Smelser, the professor who summarized the research, says in response to Vasconcellos that "self-esteem and social problems are too complicated to result in any simple conclusions. . . . When you get to looking for clear relationships as to cause and effect, particularly in areas so unclear as this one, you're not going to find them."[15]

Also, Dr. Thomas Scheff, one of the University of California professors who did the research, said that "thousands of studies have been done on self-esteem since World War II, but the results have been inconclusive."[16] One member of the Task Force was candid enough and perceptive enough to say:

The Task Force's interpretation of the UC professors' academic findings **understates the absence of a significant linkage of self-esteem and the six social problems.**[17] (Emphasis added.)

Prior to the Task Force's final report to the Governor and Legislature in June 1990 and in spite of lack of solid research support, the Chairperson, Dr. Andrew Mecca, says:

As a final project, the state Task Force is planning a state-wide conference in the Spring to share the findings and recommendations and help facilitate the transition of this work to the local task forces. (As some anthropologists have already noted, this work is just beginning!)[18]

Numerous local task forces have been established in counties throughout the state that are carrying on the mission of the State Task Force. Many other states are copycatting California. What was once relegated to the counseling office and the school classroom has entered the political arena and caught the attention of national leaders.

The Self-Esteem Movement & Christianity

This movement is harmonious with what Dobson and other self-esteem psychologists have been teaching right along. Those of us who are familiar with Dobson's self-esteem teachings and with the Task Force's self-esteem teachings cannot help but see the striking similarity. Even if Dobson disavows any interest in the Self-Esteem Task Force, the fact that they featured him and he had no objection to being featured shows that he is a fellow traveler.

Furthermore, he would agree with their definition of *self-esteem:* "Appreciating my own worth and importance, and having the character to be accountable for myself, and to act responsibly toward others." Their expanded definition of *self-esteem* easily fits into a so-called Judeo-Christian ethic:

> Being alive as a human being has an innate importance, an importance to which the Declaration of Independence refers when it declares that all people "are endowed by their Creator with certain unalienable rights. . . ." This conviction concerning the dignity of every human personality has long been a part of our nation's moral and religious heritage. Every person has a unique significance,

simply because the precious and mysterious gift of life as a human being has been given. This is an inherent value which no adversary or adversity can take away.[19]

Underneath this fine rhetoric of self-esteem and "moral and ethical responsibility" is a secular humanism which will either swallow up unwary Christians in its own ideology or eventually persecute them if they refuse to imbibe. John Vasconcellos and Mitch Saunders have said in the *Association for Humanistic Psychology* newsletter:

> The issue is *always* whether or not we believe that we humans are inherently good, trustworthy and responsible. This issue is becoming *the* central and social and political challenge of our times.[20] (Emphasis theirs.)

It is also becoming *the* spiritual issue of our times. The issue is whether Christians are going to contend for the faith once delivered to the saints or they are going to succumb to the faith of secular humanism through the deceptions of psychology and self-esteem.

Vasconcellos says that there are two competing visions in America today. One he describes as the old vision, a theological one of man as sinner. He says it's the one he grew up with. He says, "I grew up in the 1930s in a constrained, traditional Catholic family."[21] He adds, "I had been conditioned to know myself basically as a sinner, guilt-ridden and ashamed, constantly beating my breast and professing my unworthiness."[22] In contrast to the old theological vision of man, Vasconcellos speaks of the new psychological vision of man as perfectible on his own. To support this new vision, he quotes humanistic psychologist Carl Rogers, who says:

> You know, I've been practicing psychology for more than sixty years, and I have really come to believe that we human beings are innately inclined toward becoming

constructive and life-affirming and responsible and trust-worthy.[23]

Vasconcellos praises the goodness-and-trustworthiness-of-man vision over the traditional, sinfulness-of-man vision. One is a humanistic, man-centered view, while the other is a bibli-cal, God-centered view. The humanistic, man-centered view is the very foundation for the self-esteem movement. Vasconcellos says:

> It is the latter vision—that human beings are innately inclined toward good and that free, healthy people become constructive and responsible—which underlies the philosophy and work of what has been called the "self-esteem movement." There is within this movement an implicit (and increasingly explicit) intuition, an assumption—a faith, if you will—that an essential and operational relationship exists between self-esteem and responsible human behavior, both personal and social.[24]

Vasconcellos's words are enticing. On the surface they sound very moral and even religious. Indeed, they clearly express the religion of secular humanism. His underlying philosophy and faith system oppose the Gospel of Jesus Christ. More clearly than Dobson, Vasconcellos sees the difference between the self-esteem movement he espouses and the form of Christianity which he forsook. The self-esteem movement and true Christianity are contradictory in nature. One races in the direction of the self; the other moves toward God.

A psychologist from Canada, Reuven P. Bulka, who still holds some hope for bringing some concepts of psychology together with religion, clearly sees that the self-esteem movement conflicts with religion. He says:

> Having spelled out the basic principles of the selfist approach, incorporating the importance of self-esteem and other self-related affirmations, it would seem as if

the self-esteem school and religion are on a collision course. After all, the selfist school focuses on and affirms the self, whereas religion is primarily oriented around God. In religion God is the focus, and in selfist oriented psychology-philosophy, the self is the focus.[25]

He further states that "the selfist schools have not delivered on their promises, and are very often the disease of which they pretend to be the cure" and that "selfist philosophy is bankrupt, and self defeating."[26]

As we indicated earlier, Dobson's use of self-esteem is similar to that of the secular humanists. We are not saying that Dobson rejects the traditional God-centered view of man. We are saying that he is presenting a confusing message. The harmony of his self-esteem teachings with those of the Task Force and other secular humanists is undeniable to any unbiased mind and therefore confusing at least and contradictory at worst. In order to sustain and maintain his faith in God and his faith in self-esteem, he must also sustain and maintain a doublemindedness.

Members of the Self-Esteem Task Force were no doubt pleased to have such a leading, well-known and popular Christian, who has their point of view, featured as one of theirs. It will certainly help the future efforts of secular self-esteemers nationally to entice and engulf Christians from the pulpit to the pew and from Christian schools to seminaries. Secular humanists will use Christians and even promote them as long as their messages sound the same and as long as they are working for the same ostensible goal.

In a retrospective article on the self-esteem movement in America, John Rosemond says in *The Charlotte Observer* (1998):

Interestingly, rates of teen depression, drug and alcohol use (a form of withdrawal), and violence began rising sharply around the same time the "self-esteem movement began picking up steam.

Rosemond describes how, in the self-esteem movement, "'Blaming' was considered psychological assault on the right of every individual to 'good self-esteem.'" He further declares, "The rise of this psychobabble ripped off the lid of Pandora's box, and it is no wonder that the demons released have done such damage to America's children."[27]

The secular self-esteem movement is not a frontal attack with the battle-lines clearly displayed. Instead it is skillfully subversive and is truly the work, not of flesh and blood, but of principalities, powers, the rulers of darkness of this world, and spiritual wickedness in high places, just as delineated by Paul near the end of Ephesians. The sad thing is that many Christians are not alert to the dangers. More than we can number are being subtly deceived into another gospel: the gospel of self.

Education and Self-Esteem

Of course one of the primary targets of the Task Force is the schools. The schools have already been a prime place for teaching and promoting self esteem, and the Task Force has given them additional impetus, public support, and political clout. Teachers in both the public and private sector and from pre-school to graduate school have already absorbed the idea that high self-esteem and educational excellence are an inextricable pair. While teachers may have varying viewpoints about a whole host of school issues, they seem almost unanimous on the issue of self-esteem. In fact, it would be better labeled as a non-issue because of the unanimity of opinion favoring it and the obscurity and rejection of those few who oppose it.

The other end of the high-self-esteem-excellence assumption continuum is the low-self-esteem-mediocrity assumption. In other words, teachers as a whole resonate to the idea that high self-esteem brings success and low self-esteem brings failure. For at least a quarter of a century educators have been encouraging high self-esteem and discouraging low self-esteem. This high self-esteem mania/low self-esteem morbidity has become the shrine at which educators worship. It is rare to find a teacher of whatever title or level who does not subscribe to and encourage this idea. However (and this will come as a shock to many) the high/low self-esteem, success/ failure, excellence/mediocrity formula is **not** supported in the research. It is an assumption (taken for granted without proof) that remains an assumption in spite of the research findings. We will refer to this idea as *Theory 1* and will discuss two other theories of self-esteem.

If the high/low self-esteem assumption (Theory 1) were factual we would see the fruit of it in the six areas of social problems cited earlier and in the educational success/failure rates of students. We have already shown a lack of research support connecting low self-esteem and the six areas of social problems investigated by the California Task Force on Self-Esteem. With respect to education and the high/low self-esteem theory, we suggest looking at *The Excellence Commission Report*. In comparing students from different decades and countries American students fared very badly in the 1960s and 1970s. And they do not seem to have done much better in the 1980s.[28]

In the book *The Shopping Mall High School,* the senior author, Arthur Powell, gives us a picture of American schools under the domination of the high/low self-esteem theory. He says:

> Failure is anathema because success—*feeling* success—is so deeply cherished as both a goal and a means to other goals. Many teachers seem preoccupied by the psychological costs of failure and the therapeutic benefits of success. That was what one teacher was talking about when she said, "If you don't get it done, you don't fail. You don't get credit, but you don't experience failure." "The most important thing to me is to make them feel they are human beings, that they are worthwhile," another teacher emphasized. Still another's primary goals were to "build confidence, to build trust . . . I try to affirm them

as people." A math teacher prescribed "a daily dose of self-respect." And a social studies teacher explained why he didn't stress thinking skills: "I just encourage them to make the most of their ability to have pride in themselves." In all these instances, the need for students to feel success is disconnected from the idea of students mastering something taught. . . . Mastery and success are like ships that pass in the night.[29] (Emphasis his.)

Pulitzer prize-winning syndicated columnist Charles Krauthammer addresses the issue of education and self-esteem in a *Time* magazine article titled "Education: Doing Bad and Feeling Good." He says:

A standardized math test was given to 13-year-olds in six countries last year. Koreans did the best. Americans did the worst, coming in behind Spain, Britain, Ireland and Canada. Now the bad news. Besides being shown triangles and equations, the kids were shown the statement "I am good at mathematics." Koreans came last in this category. Only 23% answered yes. Americans were No. 1, with an impressive 68% in agreement.

American students may not know their math, but they have evidently absorbed the lessons of the newly fashionable self-esteem curriculum wherein kids are taught to feel good about themselves.[30]

According to one report:

The reading and writing skills of the nation's students have remained virtually unchanged in recent years and show signs of actually declining in the 1990s, according to two major studies released Tuesday by the Education Department.[31]

Reported in the same article is the following:

"Frankly there has been very little education progress made in the United States," said Education Secretary Lauro F. Cavazos, who termed the reading and writing skills of American students "dreadfully inadequate."[32]

Secretary Cavazos also said, "We should be appalled that we have placed our children in such jeopardy."[33]

A later report on the "new, improved achievement test the Educational Testing Service gave to 175,000 9-year-old and 13-year-old students in 20 countries" indicates: "The results confirm the findings of earlier math and science tests that had been criticized as being unreliable and making American students look worse than they are."[34]

Marc Tucker, president of the National Center on Education and the Economy, commented on the results, saying, "The plain fact of the matter is our performance is rotten and there are no excuses."[35]

Thanks to the great emphasis on self-esteem in the schools during the last several decades, we have this sorry state of affairs, as reported by nationally syndicated columnist James Kilpatrick:

> Over the past 30 years, one report after another has documented the sorry state of public education in the United States. . . . Everyone has heard the litany of short-comings. Thousands of children drop out of school as functional illiterates. Test scores decline. In international competitions our high school seniors usually finish in last place. In such areas as history and literature, barely half of our 11th-graders make passing scores. And so on.[36]

One publication reports:

> Of the 3.8 million eighteen-year-olds in 1988, 700,000 dropped out of high school. Another 700,000 who graduated are functionally illiterate.

In a recent survey, four out of five young adults could not summarize the main points of a newspaper article, read a bus schedule, or figure their change from a restaurant bill. In standardized tests between 1983 and 1986, American high school seniors came in last in biology among students from thirteen countries, including Hungary and Singapore. They were eleventh in chemistry and ninth in physics.

"If current trends continue," said Xerox CEO David Kearns, "U.S. businesses will have to hire a million new workers a year who can't read, write, or count. Teaching them how, and absorbing the lost productivity while they're learning, will cost industry twenty-five billion dollars a year."[37]

Dr. Diane Ravitch examined historically what happened throughout America in the social studies. She says in *The American Scholar*:

> As I examined the curriculum in different states, I came to realize that, with limited variations, there exists a national curriculum in the social studies.[38]

She tells of the development over the years from a content oriented national curriculum to a self-oriented one. She says:

> Immersion in the sociology and economics of the child's own world is supposed to build the child's self-esteem (because she studies herself and her own family), to socialize her as a member of the community, prepare her to participate in political activities, and develop her awareness of economic interdependence (by learning that the farmer grows wheat for bread, which is processed by someone else, baked by someone else, and delivered to the neighborhood grocery store by someone else). None of these assumptions has ever been empirically tested.[39]

As self-esteem first flourished in the sixties and seventies it became a driving force behind curriculum revision. Ravitch says, "It was asserted that children would build self-esteem by learning about themselves first."[40] In response to our mentioning to her the California Self-Esteem movement she says:

> I have seen evidences over the years that people in education consistently confuse the causes of self-esteem, i.e., thinking that it occurs because of talking about it, rather than realizing that it occurs as a result of having accomplished something or met a goal.[41]

Rita Kramer conducted interviews at schools across America and found, to her surprise, that self-esteem is the dominant educational theory. She describes this in her book *The Dumbing Down of American Education*. John Leo tells about it in an article in the *U.S. News & World Report* titled "The Trouble with Self-Esteem" and says:

> The Bush era turns out to be a perfect time for self-esteem programs. They cost almost nothing. They offer the light of sunny California optimism at a time of great pessimism. They are simple—easily grasped, easily spread. And in public-school systems torn by competing pressure groups, they have no natural enemies. They have only one flaw: **They are a terrible idea**.[42] (Emphasis added.)

While American education is infected with the idea that raising self-esteem will raise accomplishment, there is a second possibility: that raising accomplishment will raise self-esteem. We refer to this as *Theory 2*. If we had to choose between the two theories, we would opt for the latter.

There is another possibility (*Theory 3*), however, which is the one we believe to be the most biblical of the three. First, recall the research (Positive Illusions), consider the Bible (Proverbs 22:15: "Foolishness is bound in the heart of a child"), and assume that high self-esteem is an inherent part of man (Ephesians 5:29). Second, assume that man will be creatively deceptive to sustain his self-esteem. And third, assume that individuals generally do not need help in this area. Theory 3 encourages accomplishment without regard to self-esteem, but rather to please and glorify God. Theory 3 cannot be performed through fleshly effort, but only by the infusion of Jesus' life in believers to enable them to accomplish what is necessary and right according to God's perfect will. This idea is expressed near the end of Hebrews:

> Now the God of peace, that brought again from the dead our Lord Jesus, that great shepherd of the sheep, through the blood of the everlasting covenant, **Make you perfect in every good work to do his will, working in you that which is wellpleasing in His sight, through Jesus Christ;** to whom be glory for ever and ever. Amen (Hebrews 13:20-21). (Emphasis added.)

Self-Esteem & Self-Centeredness

There is a strong possibility that encouraging self-esteem may lead to self-sufficiency rather than dependence on God, self-deception rather than reality, pride rather than humility, and self-centeredness rather than Christ-centeredness. In a word, *narcissism*. While some would have us believe that this is an era of low self-esteem, biblical data and the research show that this is an era of narcissism. For instance, Dr. Aaron Stern has written a book titled *Me: The Narcissistic American*.[43] Also, American historian Christopher Lasch describes this era in *The Culture of Narcissism*. He says:

> Today men seek the kind of approval that applauds not their actions but their personal attributes. They wish to be not so much esteemed as admired. They crave not fame but the glamour and excitement of celebrity. They

want to be envied rather than respected. Pride and acquisitiveness, the sins of an ascendant capitalism, have given way to vanity. Most Americans would still define success as riches, fame, and power, but their actions show that they have little interest in the substance of these attainments.[44]

Daniel Yankelovich, a pollster and analyst of social trends, wrote a book entitled *New Rules: Searching for Self-Fulfillment in a World Turned Upside Down.* In it he documents changes that have occurred in our society. He describes "the struggle for self-fulfillment" as "the leading edge of a genuine cultural revolution." He claims, "It is moving our industrial civilization toward a new phase of human experience."[45] In describing the new rules, Yankelovich says:

> In their extreme form, the new rules simply turn the old ones on their head, and in place of the old self-denial ethic we find people who refuse to deny *anything* to themselves.[46]

The cover of the book states:

> *New Rules* is about that 80 percent of Americans now committed to one degree or another to the search for self-fulfillment, at the expense of the older, self-denying ethic of earlier years.[47]

The new formula for society has become faith in a cause and effect relationship between a high amount of self-love and self-esteem leading to health, wealth, and happiness. One can see in *New Rules* that humanistic psychology is the narcissism of our culture. Even well-known humanistic psychologist Rollo May says of Yankelovich's conclusions, "I can see he is right."[48]

It is our belief that, in the main, a focus on high/low self-esteem, success/failure, excellence/mediocrity theory (Theory 1) will lead to just the opposite of what it hopes to produce with respect to social problems, educational excellence, and other areas of life. Theory 2 is a better possibility, but instead of having no tangible basis for high self-esteem as in Theory 1, it is still subject to the natural, human inclination toward narcissism. Theory 3, which focuses on accomplishments through Christ's enabling, but without regard to enhancing self-esteem, will be in harmony with Scripture.

The lack of support in the research literature for Theory 1 should lead to testing Theory 2. Theory 2 existed before the current self-esteem era and its results surpass those of Theory 1. However, Theory 3 can certainly be seen from Scripture and in the actual practice and writings of believers before the present century. For instance, Lasch reminds us:

> The true Christian, according to Calvinistic conceptions of an honorable and godly existence, bore both good fortune and bad with equanimity, contenting himself with what came to his lot. "This he had learned to doe," said John Cotton, "if God prosper him he had learned not to be puffed up, and if he should be exposed to want, he could do it without murmuring. It is the same act of unbeleefe, that makes a man murmure in crosses, which puffes him up in prosperity."[49]

As indicated earlier, high self-esteem is the natural state of children and adults. A child's ego, in the main, is naturally robust and is not in constant need of reinforcement. The children or adults who are in a state of collapse are the exception, not the rule. High self-esteem is a natural state of man; self deprecation is not.

Krauthammer addresses the issue of self-love in an article titled "More Self-Love Isn't the Answer." He says:

> The ideology of self-love enjoyed currency during the '70s as a form of psychic recreation for the Me Generation. It has now been resurrected as a cure for the social pathologies of the '80s, for the drug and other behavioral

epidemics that ravage the nation and particularly the inner cities. The conventional wisdom is that people are acting so self-destructively because of an absence of self-worth. Until they can learn to love themselves, they will continue to damage both themselves and others.[50]

After giving an example and discussing it, Krauthammer says:

Indeed, today's conventional wisdom that drug abuse and alcoholism and sexual irresponsibility come from an absence of self-worth seems to me to be precisely wrong. Drugs and sex and alcohol have but one thing in common: They yield intense and immediate pleasure. That is why people do them. Indulgence in what used to be called vices is an act of excessive self-love.[51]

Krauthammer begins his article as follows:

So the Atlanta cabby tells his fare—Professor Allan Bloom—that he has just gotten out of prison where, happily, with the help of psychotherapy, he "found his identity and learned to like himself." Observes Bloom: "A generation earlier he would have found God and learned to despise himself."[52]

Dr. Allan Bloom has an interesting subtitle for his book *The Closing of the American Mind*. The subtitle is: *How Higher Education Has Failed Democracy and Impoverished the Souls of Today's Students*. Bloom discusses the self and says:

For us the most revealing and delightful distinction—because it is so unconscious of its wickedness—is between inner-directed and other-directed, with the former taken to be unqualifiedly good. Of course, we are told, the healthy inner-directed person will really take care for others. To which I can only respond: If you can believe that, you can believe anything.[53] (Emphasis his.)

The subtitle of the Wallachs' book *Psychology's Sanction for Selfishness* is *The Error of Egoism in Theory and Therapy*. In their book they say:

> We have seen in earlier chapters how selfishness is promoted by urging realization and expression of the self. Those who have done this urging—particularly Horney, Fromm, Maslow, and Rogers—have held that if people are really actualizing themselves, they will in fact be good to one another. But, as we have discussed, this cannot keep the encouragement to focus on oneself and one's own development from supporting concern for self in contrast to concern for others. Far as it was from their intention, these psychologists inevitably promote selfishness by asking us to realize ourselves, to love ourselves, to view the environment as a means for our own self-actualizing ends, and to consider whether something will contribute to our own development as the only real criterion for what we should do.[54]

While it may not be the intent of self-esteemers to promote selfishness or egoism, we believe it is an inevitable result. In response to a letter, the Wallachs' say:

> It may well be that one factor in people's involvement in substance abuse, crime, teenage pregnancy, and welfare dependency is their low opinion of their own lives, their low expectations of what they could accomplish even if they behaved differently. But the way to remedy that would not seem to be to attack their feelings about themselves, but to attack the actual conditions that are responsible for these feelings. More often than not, the feelings are an accurate reflection of present conditions. So long as people don't really have much to hope for,

attempting to manipulate their psychological states instead of their actual circumstances—even assuming it could be done—would seem at best just one more kind of opiate for the masses. It seems to us that what is needed is not further turning inward, not still more concern with our feelings about ourselves, but rather turning outward, concern with the environment we create for one another.[55]

Even though one primary goal of self-esteem is to feel good enough about oneself in order to become other-centered, there is no guarantee that people will naturally move from self-esteem to other-centeredness. Just looking at our society and considering the growing influence of these teachings since the days of Adler and Maslow should lead one to have a dubious view of such expectations.

Highly influential humanistic psychologists reject the idea that self-actualizing or self-esteem leads to selfishness or egoism. However, that can be the result of any system that emphasizes the self, presupposes the goodness of the human, and claims that people will develop their highest potential if so-called needs are met. In a chapter titled "Maslow's Other Child," Adrianne Aron describes how Maslow's teachings led to the hippie movement. She says:

To examine some of the more menacing aspects of a pursuit of self-actualization that disregards political and ethical matters, I shall discuss here the dominant social pattern of the hippie movement in its early days. In the hippie pattern Maslow's dream of a compassionate, reciprocal, empathic, high-synergy scheme of interpersonal relations gets lost behind a reality of human exploitation. Where the theorist prescribed self-actualization the hippies produced mainly self-indulgence. Yet, I shall argue, the hippie result is not alien to the Maslovian theory, for when the relationship between self and society is left undefined and unattended by a theory of self-development, one social pattern is as likely to emerge as another.[56]

Maslow's dream for a Utopia inhabited with self-actualized persons of high self-esteem was realized in the Haight-Asbury district of San Francisco, as the flower children of the sixties took his theories to heart and lived a life of free love and self-gratification.[57] Maslow did not teach self-indulgence, but that can be the result of any system which emphasizes the self, presupposes the goodness of the human, and claims that people will develop their highest potential if so-called needs are met.

Dr. William R. Coulson, a former colleague of Rogers and Maslow, says that in his later years Maslow did not agree with much of what he had theorized in his earlier years. Coulson quotes from the second edition of *Motivation and Personality*:

> . . . the high scorers in my test of dominance-feeling or self-esteem were more apt to come late to appointments with the experimenter, to be less respectful, more casual, more forward, more condescending, less tense, anxious, and worried, more apt to accept an offered cigarette, much more apt to make themselves comfortable without bidding or invitation.

> **The stronger [high self-esteem] woman is much more apt to be pagan, permissive, and accepting in all sexual realms. She is less apt to be a virgin. . . more apt to have had sexual relations with more than one man. . . .**[58] (Emphasis added.)

In other words, Maslow found that satisfying the so-called self-esteem needs did **not** produce the desired results. And that is the problem with so many of the self theories. They begin with fallen flesh and simply end up with another face of fallen flesh. Dobson and Christians who follow him seem to ignore these results.

In his article "The Social Usefulness of Self-Esteem: A Skeptical View" in the October, 1998 issue of *The Harvard Mental Health Letter,* Dr. Robyn Dawes says:

> Hidden lack of self-esteem is the New Age psychologist's ether. The ether was a substance that was supposed to fill all space as a vehicle for the travel of light waves. It proved undetectable, and the concept was discarded when Einstein introduced the special theory of relativity. A belief in undetected low self-esteem as a cause of undesirable behavior is even less plausible; all the available evidence directly contradicts it.[59]

Dawes sums up the research on self-esteem at the end of his article with these words: "The false belief in self-esteem as a major force for good can be not just potentially but actually harmful."[60]

Few Christians suspect that raising self-esteem might be harmful; even fewer understand the actual harm that elevated self-esteem does to one's spiritual life. They believe the gospel of self-esteem and will have a difficult time separating this erroneous belief from their faith in God, because influential teachers, such as Dobson, have convincingly connected God with high self-esteem.

8

God and Self-Esteem

While advocating self-esteem and self-worth, Dobson adamantly points out the error of self-centeredness. In response to a question about the book *Jonathan Livingston Seagull*, Dobson rightly responds:

> This book expressed a damaging philosophy that became popular about eight years ago, which can be summarized by the phrase "Do your own thing." It means, in brief, that I'm protecting my own self-interests and will do whatever suits my fancy, regardless of the needs of others or the moral values of my society.[1]

Dobson sees how contrary that is to the Christian message and says:

> It is my conviction that these messages are directly contradictory to the essence of Christianity which puts its emphasis on giving, sharing, caring, loving, turning the other cheek, going the second mile, and accepting God's commandments.[2]

But do any psychological self-esteem, self-acceptance, and self-love teachings reflect "the essence of Christianity"? Along with secular humanistic psychologists, Dobson believes that self-esteem, self-worth, and self-acceptance will lead to personal and social responsibility—that self-esteem is almost equivalent to giving, sharing, caring, and loving. However, the essence of Christianity is not "giving, sharing, caring, loving" as a result of loving, accepting, and esteeming self. One can give, share, care and love that way and be eternally lost. The essence of Christianity is "Christ in you, the hope of glory," not self-improvement or gaining self-esteem. It is "giving, sharing, caring, loving, turning the other cheek, going the second mile," and obeying God's commandments because of Christ—because of what He has done and is doing in the life of the believer.

For Dobson, things get reversed. Even if he does not intend it, the focus always slips back to the advantage for the self. He says:

> When the family conforms to God's blueprint, then self-esteem is available for everyone—which satisfies romantic aspirations—which abolishes loneliness, isolation, and boredom—which contributes to sexual fulfillment—which binds the marriage together in fidelity—which provides security for children—which gives parents a sense of purpose—which contributes to self-esteem once more.[3]

Thus self-esteem becomes the reason to obey God. The goal of obedience becomes subtly swerved from a desire to please God to a desire to gain personal advantages. But if love and obedience for God are for personal (selfish) pragmatic reasons, rather than for biblical reasons, what happens when romantic aspirations are not satisfied and isolation is increased and there is no sexual fulfillment as a direct result of obedience to Christ? Such a promise for self-esteem and personal fulfillment could not have kept the church alive throughout centuries of persecution.

Confidence in Self or God

Self-confidence and self-esteem go together. Dobson stresses the importance of self-confidence throughout his books. However, he confuses the source of confidence when he attempts to make self-confidence sound biblical. He quotes a young man saying:

> I've learned that God made everybody the way they are for a reason, and He doesn't make mistakes. I've met a few people who understood that principle and refused to let their [physical] imperfections bother them.[4]

Then the young man shares a beautiful testimony about a girl who has a crippling disease for which she must wear leg braces. He says:

> She is such a glory to God, because she knows that she's supposed to be like that. . . . But people often get so concerned with the way they look that they fail to understand that God can use them just the way they are. God has a purpose for each one of us, and it's our duty to find out what His purposes are and then to fulfill them.[5] (Emphasis his.)

Dobson responds: "That's the secret of self-confidence."[6] Dobson reduces a God honoring and God-centered declaration to self-confidence. Why is that not confidence in God and in His faithfulness rather than confidence in self?

Paul certainly would not have made such a remark, for he declared that he put no confidence in self. His confidence was in the Lord. However, when psychology is the foundation, all roads eventually lead back to self, even for those who give a nod to God or use Him to build up the self.

For Dobson the answer to lack of confidence is self-confidence. He continues:

This is a principle that I would like all our readers to understand. You may think you have no ability or skills, but your real problem is that you merely lack *confidence*.[7] (Emphasis his.)

The answer to feeling inferior and inadequate according to Dobson is found in identifying hidden abilities and cultivating them.[8] And then he declares: "With a little confidence you can achieve something that will make you proud of yourself."[9] All of this sounds like the advice of the world and the goal of the world, not the advice of the Bible or the goal of the Christian life. Paul counted all of his past achievements based on his own confidence "dung." But as a called minister of the Gospel, Paul confesses: "Not that we are sufficient of ourselves to think any thing as of ourselves; but our sufficiency is of God" (2 Corinthians 3:5).

However, Dobson brings Jesus into the picture, not as our sufficiency, but as someone who can help a person with self-confidence. In response to one youth's declaration that Jesus is there "to give me confidence" and that he depends on "partnership with God," Dobson speaks of the importance of God being involved. But there's a difference between self-confidence and confidence in God. Because of the oneness of believers with their Lord, confidence for whatever task He assigns comes from His enabling. After all, He is the One who made and gifts people. He is the one who lives in and empowers believers to do every good work (Hebrews 13:20-21). Therefore, we must constantly teach our children to find their confidence in Him.

Dobson's Doctrine of Man

Dobson repeatedly assures his readers and listeners that he is not a theologian. He especially avoids doctrinal issues which may be controversial between denominations. Nevertheless, he teaches a doctrine of man which is both psychological and theological. In Dobson's theology man is central and God serves to help people overcome inferiority and develop self-esteem and self-acceptance.

An example of his theological doctrine of man can be seen in two of Dobson's statements about the human spirit. In *Hide or Seek* Dobson declares:

> The human spirit is exceedingly fragile at all ages and must be handled with care. It involves a person's view of himself, his personal worth, and the emotional factors to which this book is dedicated.[10]

According to Dobson the human spirit is "fragile" and is intrinsically tied to self-esteem. He says:

> A parent can damage his child's spirit very easily—by ridicule, disrespect, threats to withdraw love, and by verbal rejection. Anything that depreciates his self-esteem is costly to his spirit.[11]

Dobson seems to equate the human spirit and self-esteem. Earlier in the same book he says:

> It is a wise parent who understands that self-esteem is the most fragile characteristic in human nature, and once broken, its reconstruction is more difficult than repairing Humpty Dumpty.[12]

One could almost substitute the term *self-esteem* with *spirit* here and he would be saying the same thing. Indeed, Dobson defines each with the other and both as exceedingly fragile. It does not seem to bother him that no passage in Scripture equates self-esteem and the human spirit. Nor does Scripture give us any notion of the spirit as "fragile."

Furthermore, according to Dobson, the human spirit is separate from the will. In *The Strong-Willed Child*, he says:

On the other hand (and let me give this paragraph the strongest possible emphasis), the *spirit* of a child is a million times more vulnerable than his will. It is a delicate flower than can be crushed and broken all too easily (and even unintentionally). The spirit, as I have defined it, relates to the self-esteem or the personal worth that a child feels. It is *the* most fragile characteristic in human nature, being particularly vulnerable to rejection and ridicule and failure.[13] (Emphasis his.)

Notice that Dobson did not find his definition in the Bible. He says, "The spirit, **as I have defined it**, relates to self-esteem or the personal worth that a child feels."[14] (Emphasis added.) His definition comes from his psychological viewpoint rather than from the Bible. And whenever anyone speaks of the spirit of a person he is knee-deep in theology. He is talking about spiritual matters. Whether he wants to or not he is revealing his theology.

Besides Dobson's idea of spirit being separate from the will (whatever that means), it appears that the spirit is to remain intact, for Dobson asks, "How, then are we to shape the will while preserving the spirit intact?"[15] Does this mean that when Paul declared, "I am crucified with Christ," his spirit need not be included in the crucifixion? Does this mean that the spirit of an unbeliever is exempt from the total depravity of man? Does this mean that a person's spirit is not tainted with sin?

Dobson continues to separate spirit from will. He says:

To repeat, our guiding purpose is to shape the child's will without breaking his spirit. This dual objective is outlined for us throughout the Scriptures, but is specifically stated in two important references.[16]

He then cites 1 Timothy 3:4-5 for *"Shaping the Will"* and Ephesians 6:4 for *"Preserving the Spirit."*

One that ruleth well his own house, having his children in subjection with all gravity; (For if a man know not how to rule his own house, how shall he take care of the church of God?) (1 Timothy 3:4-5).

And, ye fathers, provoke not your children to wrath: but bring them up in the nurture and admonition of the Lord (Ephesians 6:4).

However, these verses do not speak of will and spirit, but what to do with the child. It would have been better to start with such biblical passages for wisdom and instructions in child rearing rather than with psychology.

What Bible passage relates the human spirit to self-esteem? We find none. *The Expanded Vine's Expository Dictionary of New Testament Words* does not list self-esteem under the expanded definition of spirit. *Vine's Dictionary* includes such definitions as "the immaterial, invisible part of man" (which would by this definition include the will or volition); "the sentient element in man, that by which he perceives, reflects, feels, desires" as in 1 Corinthians 2:11; and "purpose, aim. . . character . . . moral qualities. . . the inward man."[17]

Paul lists nothing that remotely sounds like self-esteem or self-worth when he lists the activities resulting from being "renewed in the spirit of your mind" (Ephesians 4:23-32). Being "renewed in the spirit of your mind" is moving from a worldly mind-set to a mind-set that has been rejuvenated by Christ. It is that inner work which God does as a believer puts off the ways of his old self (v. 22) and puts on "the new man, which after God is created in righteousness and true holiness" (v. 24). The spirit of man has a great deal to do with volition and direction. And while the unregenerate human spirit may be full of deceitful lusts and therefore include self-referencing activities such as self-love and self-esteem, this does not make the human spirit equivalent to self-esteem.

Man-Centered Gospel

Dobson presents a mixed message, the psychological message of the world and principles from Christianity that seem to fit. Therefore he presents a man-centered gospel rather than a Christ-centered Gospel. The focus is on the human rather than on God. The emphasis is on so-called emotional needs. The reason for behaving in a certain way appears to be more for human benefit than to please God. The need for salvation is human hurts and human worth rather than because of man's total depravity and God's magnificent mercy and grace.

Dobson seems to make no clear delineation between the believer and the unbeliever as far as diagnosis (inferiority, low self-esteem) and remedy (compensation, high self-esteem). However, from a biblical point of view there is a gigantic difference between the saved and the unsaved, and it's not based on some kind of level of self-esteem.

Dobson makes a number of statements about God in relation to his self-esteem teachings. However, he has no scriptural basis for his declarations about self-esteem, self-worth, or self-love. And since he does not intend to be a theologian but rather a psychologist, he probably does not feel the need to base his work on the Bible. In correspondence from the Focus on the Family ministry, one of his employees says:

> Dr. Dobson has made a deliberate decision to direct the attention of our ministry away from matters of biblical interpretation and theology, choosing instead to concentrate our efforts exclusively on family-related topics.[18]

However such a decision does not free an avowed Christian ministry to the family from basing its teachings on Scripture. It is an admission to placing the Bible in a secondary position to the psychological wisdom of men. Apparently Dobson does not agree that the Bible is sufficient for understanding human nature and guiding behavior.

Even though Dobson "has made a deliberate decision to direct the attention of [his] ministry away from matters of biblical interpretation and theology," he claims that the underlying principles of his teachings "originated with the inspired biblical writers who gave us the foundation for all relationships in the home."[19] While some of the underlying principles may have originated with the Bible, much of what he writes and says originated from the unregenerate minds of psychologists who claim to be scientists, even though their theories have more to do with man-centered religion than with science.

Even though Dobson has made a deliberate decision to avoid theology and biblical interpretation, he does speak and write about God, especially in reference to his own psychological ideas. We will look at a few of his statements about God and man.

Image of God

As with other Christian self-esteemers, Dobson contends that God Himself intends that every person have a genuine sense of self-worth. He says:

> *Every* child is entitled to hold up his head, not in haughtiness and pride, but in confidence and security. This is the concept of human worth intended by our Creator. How foolish for us to doubt our value when He formed us in His own image![20] (Emphasis his.)

From this statement one can see that Dobson relates human worth with a person being "entitled to hold up his head. . . in confidence and security." He equates self-worth and self-esteem in the same way he equates feelings of inferiority, self-doubt, and low self-esteem. Elsewhere he uses the terms *self-worth*, *worthy*, and *worthiness* interchangeably.[21]

Should human beings indulge in feelings of self-worth and self-esteem because they are created in God's image? Or was there another purpose for being created in the image of God, that is, to reflect Him and live in relationship to Him? Being created in the image of God presupposes responsibility to Him.

Gordon Clark's remarks about man in the image of God do not make one feel worthy, but rather responsible. He asks, "What became of the image of God when Adam fell? . . . Did man cease to be God's image?" Then he answers:

> No; man did not cease to be God's image. Paradoxical though it may seem, man could not be a sinner at all, even now, if he were not still God's image. Sinning presupposes rationality and voluntary decision. Animals cannot sin. Sin therefore requires God's image because man is responsible for his sins. If there were no responsibility, there could be nothing properly called sin. Sin is an offense against God, and God calls us to account. If we were not answerable to God, repentance would be useless, indeed impossible nonsense. Reprobation and hell would also be impossible; for God has made responsibility a function of knowledge. . . . Sin does not eradicate the image; but it certainly causes a malfunctioning.[22]

Does a correct view of what it means to be in the image of God make us feel profound self-worth? Or does it call us to the cross, not only for salvation, but for sanctification as well?

Since the original image was marred, the Father is in the process of conforming His children into the image of His dear Son. And He uses all kinds of circumstances to complete the task (Romans 8:29). Also Paul encourages believers to look at the Lord rather than at themselves when he says:

> But we all, with open face beholding as in a glass the glory of the Lord, are changed into the same image from glory to glory, even as by the Spirit of the Lord (2 Corinthians 3:18).

In comparison with such glory, esteeming oneself and feeling valuable seem puny and picayunish.

Faith for Ego Satisfaction?

Dobson seems to reduce the goal of faith to ego satisfaction, for he says:

> I believe *the* most valuable contribution a parent can make to his child is to instill in him a genuine faith in God. What greater ego satisfaction could there be than knowing that the Creator of the Universe is acquainted with me, personally? That He values me more than the possessions of the entire world.[23] (Emphasis his.)

It is amazing how the realization that "the Creator of the Universe is acquainted with me, personally" can so quickly plunge into "greater ego satisfaction." One would think that such an awesome revelation would humble a person. To think that God cares about me personally should open the floodgates of praise and adoration for Him, rather than satisfaction with self. When one knows the intimacy and the grandeur of relationship with God the Father through Jesus Christ, self is lost in a sea of love and amazement. Ego fades and self identifies with the cross of Christ.

Jesus did not die so that people can enjoy ego satisfaction. He died to save them from their sins and to give them new life. Saving faith in God includes trusting and obeying God. There is no saint in the Bible who reduced faith in God to ego satisfaction. A quick look at Hebrews 11 shows the intense devotion for God that comes from valid faith in Him. While there is joy in serving Jesus and love and peace with God, one cannot equate that with ego satisfaction. The fruit of the spirit emphasizes the relationship with Christ, not self, for Jesus said, "Without me you can do nothing" (John 15:5). And to be absolutely frank, without Him we **are** nothing. With Him we are containers, servants, friends, children, and brothers. But, these are all terms of relationship, not ego satisfaction. They are terms of dependence on God, not independent self-esteem or personal worth.

In that same statement which related faith in God to ego satisfaction, Dobson declares that God "values me more than the possessions of the entire world."[24] Isn't that a bit presumptuous? Instead, Christians should value God "more than the possessions of the entire world." While Jesus does say that those who were listening to him were worth more than many sparrows, there is no Bible reference that says that one person is worth "more than the possessions of the entire world."

Value and worth are always attributed by someone for someone or something, not something intrinsically belonging to anyone but God. After expanding the above quotation, Dobson continues by saying, "This is self-esteem at its richest, not dependent on the whims of birth. . . ."[25] One wonders how the phrase "whims of birth" lines up with Psalm 139.

Throughout the annals of Scripture it is nearly impossible to find men of faith who continued in self-esteem. Moses evidenced a bit of self-esteem when he sought to set matters straight in Egypt and slew a man. However, God could not use him until all confidence in self had evaporated in the desert during the forty years he tended Jethro's sheep. When God called him, Moses did not even have confidence to speak for God. But instead of raising his self-confidence and his self-esteem, God said, "I will be with thee" (Exodus 3). In the account of Aaron and Miriam speaking against Moses during their own period of elevated self-esteem, comes this parenthetical statement: "Now the man Moses was very meek, above all the men which were upon the face of the earth" (Numbers 12:3). Faith and meekness go together in Scripture, not faith and self-esteem. Jesus referred to Himself as "meek and lowly in heart" (Matthew 11:29).

Does the Bible Connect Self-Esteem with Salvation?

Dobson evidently believes that salvation is a reason for self-esteem. He says:

> . . . what greater source of self-esteem can there be than to know that Jesus would have died for him if he were the only human being on earth.[26]

Should salvation cause a person to esteem himself or to esteem Christ? When one considers why Jesus had to die to save sinners, there is little room for self-esteem. Paul describes every unsaved person's horrible condition as "alienated and enemies in your mind by wicked works" (Colossians 1:21), "dead in trespasses and sins," "children of disobedience," "fulfilling the desires of the flesh and of the mind," and "children of wrath" (Ephesians 2:1-3). Then Paul declares, "But God, who is rich in mercy, for his great love wherewith he loved us, even when we were dead in sins, hath quickened us together with Christ (by grace ye are saved)" (Ephesians 2:4-5). Salvation rests on God's abounding grace, not on personal worth.

Dr. Trevor Craigen questions the doctrine of redemption being used "to proclaim that man is something worth dying for, and that one may now attribute to himself dignity, worth and significance or may see himself as something worthwhile." He says:

> In Scripture no context presenting the wonder and grandeur of salvation even remotely suggests or attempts to apply the doctrine in such a way so that anyone may now validly conclude himself to be worth dying for, or himself to be worthwhile and significant. . . . Salvation is, in all of its aspects, a testimony of the grace of God toward those who were unworthy of eternal life and of His love. Salvation signifies, not the worth of man, but the sinfulness of man.[27]

The Bible says that Jesus died to save sinners. He saved us because of our sin and utter depravity, not because of our goodness, value and worth. The Bible says, "Christ died for the ungodly" (Romans 5:6). Even children need to be taught a proper biblical view of the goodness of God and the depravity of man. And, to set up a hypothetical situation, that "Jesus would have died for him if he were the only human being on earth," is to depart from Scripture and to indulge in speculation. Even if that were so, it would not give just cause for self-esteem. Instead, it would show forth the mystery of God's mercy and grace.

The foundational meaning of the word *grace* is unmerited favor. How can we be saved by grace and not that of ourselves (Ephesians 2:8) if we are of independent value and worth? If we are of value and worth in ourselves, then it is not grace. It is a business transaction. If we are of intrinsic value and worth, Jesus' death was not a sacrifice but a shrewd bargain. Whenever we move from the mercy and grace of God in terms of salvation and put independent value on ourselves, we are saying that people deserve to be saved, because they are worth it. Or people deserve to be loved by God, because they are lovable and worth His love.

Vine's Dictionary says this about God's love for man:

> In respect of *agapao* as used of God, it expresses the deep and constant love and interest of a perfect Being towards entirely unworthy objects. . . ."[28]

When God chooses out of His own boundless love to place value on a human being, the reasons are resident within Himself, not in the person He has chosen to love. In his book *The Danger of Self-Love*, Paul Brownback declares:

> Whatever our worth may be, whatever capacities we may have, whatever may be accomplished through them, as we recognize that everything of worth finds its ultimate source in God and depends on Him for life and meaning

and fruitfulness, the appropriate response is not self-esteem but adoration of the God who is the source of all.[29]

Jesus said, "Blessed are the poor in spirit: for theirs is the kingdom of heaven" (Matthew 5:3). Charles Spurgeon says that Jesus "is speaking of a poverty of spirit, a lowliness of heart, an absence of self-esteem."[30] Matthew Henry says that to be "poor in spirit" is:

> To be humble and lowly in our own eyes. To be *poor in spirit*, is to think meanly of ourselves, of what we are, and have, and do; it is to be as little children in our opinion of ourselves. Paul was rich in *spirituals*, excelling most in gifts and graces, and yet *poor in spirit, the least of the apostles*, less than the least of all saints, and *nothing* in his own account. It is to be willing to make ourselves cheap [of little worth], and mean [lowly], and little, to do good; to *become all things to all men*. It is to acknowledge that God is great, and we are mean [lowly]; that he is holy and we are sinful; that he is all and we are nothing. . . . To come off from all confidence in our own righteousness and strength, that we may depend only upon the merit of Christ and the spirit and grace of Christ. That *broken and contrite spirit* with which the publican cried for mercy to a poor sinner, is the poverty of spirit. We must call ourselves poor, because we are always in want of God's grace. . . . [31] (Emphasis his.)

That is quite the opposite of what Adler, Maslow, and Rogers would say. In fact, they would have a big problem with such a statement and criticize Christians for teaching such doctrines. Nevertheless, Jesus did **not** say: "Blessed are those who have high self-esteem," or "Blessed are they who have replaced inferiority feelings with high self-esteem," or "Blessed are they who have a healthy sense of self-worth and self-acceptance." The message of the Bible is **not** the same as the humanistic message of the purveyors of self-esteem.

To use God's saving grace to bolster up a secular concept dredged out of the cistern of theories and therapies devised by men who opposed the God of the Bible is preposterous. It totally detracts from the reality of salvation and the meaning of redemption. It ends in self and does not lead to a biblical understanding of what it means to be a child of God. Craigen explains it this way:

> To be sure, one who has professed faith in Christ, on the basis of special revelation, (1) has authority to call himself a child of God; (2) knows that he has eternal life; and (3) acknowledges that he is a participant in a redemptive program that leads to glorification. These benefits and privileges are clearly presented in Scripture. Immediately there devolves upon the believer, however, those obligations and responsibilities consistent with the character, conduct, and life of one who is, by the grace of God, a new creation. **Acceptance of biblical revelation's declarations of what one is in Christ leads not to introspective affirmations of worth and significance but to somber reflection upon progress in sanctification.**[32] (Emphasis added.)

To say that Christ died for me because I'm worth it or to say that I can have high self-esteem because He died for me changes the Gospel of Jesus Christ to a gospel of self. If the gospel of self-esteem falls into the category of "another gospel," we have as much reason to fear for Christians as Paul feared when he wrote:

> But I fear, lest by any means, as the serpent beguiled Eve through his subtilty, so your minds should be corrupted from the simplicity that is in Christ. For if he that cometh preacheth another Jesus, whom we have not preached, or if ye receive another spirit, which ye have

not received, or another gospel, which ye have not accepted, ye might well bear with him (2 Corinthians 11:3-4).

The Gospel of Christ proclaims the grace of God extended to a poor sinner, and when that sinner is redeemed by the blood of the lamb he receives new life in Christ. Throughout the ages the redeemed responded by worshiping, honoring, and serving the Lord, **not** by esteeming themselves. Self-esteem teachers reduce the cross of Christ to a bridge between the island of inferiority and low self-esteem to the mainland of confidence and high self-esteem. But, the Bible does not teach that people suffer from low self-esteem; it says that they suffer from sin and its consequences. The cross of Christ is the answer to sin, not the bridge to high self-esteem.

Worm Theology

Dobson's support for his self-esteem theology can be seen in the Epilogue of his book *Hide or Seek*. Since the Epilogue is only in the revised edition, we assume that it is Dobson's purpose to answer criticism directed at his earlier edition. In this section he mentions "speaking to a sizable audience in Boston." He says that after his talk an elderly lady who had been a missionary questioned what he had said. Dobson quotes her as saying, "God wants me to think of myself as being no better than a worm."[33] Dobson responds:

> Unfortunately, this fragile missionary (and thousands of other Christians) had been taught that she was worthless. But that teaching did not come from the Scriptures. Jesus did not leave His throne in heaven to die for the "worms" of the world. His sacrifice was intended for that little woman, and for me and all of His followers, whom He is not embarrassed to call brothers. What a concept! If Jesus is now my brother, then that puts me in the family

of God, and guarantees that I will outlive the universe itself. And that, friends, is what I call genuine self-esteem![34]

Contained within this one paragraph is Dobson's doctrine of who man is and the sacrifice that God paid. Contained within this Epilogue is Dobson's justification for his self-esteem teachings. Thus his self-esteem position succeeds or fails based upon what he says in this section.

Dobson apparently objects to "worm" theology, even though it is based on solid biblical doctrine. Worm theology says that people are not worthy in themselves to receive the bountiful love and grace of God. There is no deserving, only grateful receiving. Thus there is no room for self-esteem because the praise and glory go to God. Dobson is absolutely wrong when he says, "Jesus did not leave His throne in heaven to die for the 'worms' of the world." If one looks at the description of the lost in Scripture, they look more like worms than deserving candidates for God's love. For instance:

The heart is deceitful above all things, and desperately wicked; who can know it? (Jeremiah 17:9).

But we are all as an unclean thing, and all our righteousnesses are as filthy rags; and we all do fade as a leaf; and our iniquities, like the wind, have taken us away (Isaiah 64:6).

As it is written, There is none righteous, no, not one: There is none that understandeth, there is none that seeketh after God. They are all gone out of the way, they are together become unprofitable; there is none that doeth good, no, not one (Romans 3:10-12).

For all have sinned, and come short of the glory of God (Romans 3:23).

For I know that in me (that is, in my flesh,) dwelleth no good thing: for to will is present with me; but how to perform that which is good I find not (Romans 7:18).

. . . by nature we are the children of wrath (Eph. 2:3).

Considering these and other passages, what other conclusions could one come to? Dobson apparently rejects the doctrine of total depravity and credits man for his salvation. Otherwise there would be no cause for esteeming self, only reason to glorify God.

Is Dobson suggesting that man was worth the price that God paid for him? If Dobson thinks so, it only makes sense from a secular humanistic framework, but certainly not from a biblical point of view. Such a transaction would be paying for merchandise that is worth the price, but the Bible reveals that salvation is by grace alone and not by the addition of any merit or intrinsic worth of the individual who is saved.

We assume Dobson is referring to Hebrews 2:11 when he says:

His sacrifice was intended for that little woman, and for me and all of His followers, whom He is not embarrassed to call brothers. What a concept! If Jesus is now my brother, then that puts me in the family of God, and guarantees that I will outlive the universe itself. And that, friends, is what I call genuine self-esteem![35]

Hebrews 2:11 says: "For both he that sanctifieth and they who are sanctified are all of one: for which cause he is not ashamed to call them brethren." Dobson says this is evidence for "genuine self-esteem." He apparently means that Christ's sacrificial death for us and His bringing us into the family of God are the basis for "genuine self-esteem." In other words, because we are in the family of God we have reason to esteem self. Dobson's connection of self-esteem to being undeservedly placed in the family of God through Christ taking the penalty is astonishing! Instead of giving all the glory to God, self is esteemed.

There may be some theologian who supports Dobson's "genuine self-esteem" notion based upon Hebrews 2:11. If so, we invite Dobson to indicate this to us. Unfortunately, Dobson glibly proclaims the idea, but never supports it. We do not require him to be a theologian. We only ask that he be biblical. In this instance he has failed to make the connection between self-esteem and Hebrews 2:11. And, he has failed to show any theologians who make such a connection. Who man is and the price God paid to redeem him are important biblical doctrines—too important to be dealt with on the basis of Dobson's personal opinion unsupported by biblical exegesis.

A Confused Message

The Bible teaches that Jesus saves people from the domination of sin and the tyranny of the self. Dobson says:

> Why do I stress the role of the Christian faith so strongly in reference to our children's self-esteem and worthiness? Because this belief offers the only way of life which can free us from the tyranny of the self.[36]

According to the Bible the tyranny of the self is dealt with at the cross. However, Dobson stresses the idea of a cross that deals with the tyranny of low self-esteem, since his brand of Christian faith is supposed to raise self-esteem and give a person a great sense of self-worth. In humanistic psychology, the tyranny of the self is reduced by meeting the so-called needs of Maslow's hierarchy, such as self-worth and self-esteem. Thus Dobson seems to be preaching two messages: the Christian message and the humanistic psychological message.

The Bible teaches that the sinful self is initially dealt with by the cross of Christ and that believers are thereafter enabled to put off the old self by denying it, by not letting self rule. But

Dobson is not referring to putting the self to death or to denying the self. Instead he encourages faith in God to gain self-esteem, worthiness, and ego satisfaction.

In attempting to add some biblical ideas to the end of the revised version of *Hide or Seek*, Dobson seems to contradict himself. All through the book he encourages parents to help their children develop self-esteem. But then suddenly, he says that the more the need for self-esteem is gratified, the more demanding it becomes. And that certainly makes sense. In fact one psychologist says:

> Self-esteem, after all, is the type of feeling that needs constant reinforcement, and it almost feeds on itself. The more that you have of it, the more you are likely to need and want. It is the emotional counterpart of the quest for wealth. When one has acquired some amount of wealth, it only brings with it an escalated desire to acquire even more.[37]

Of course from a biblical perspective that sounds like lust. But, it is a bit confusing for Dobson to insert this idea because it contradicts the rest of his book. The contradiction comes because he is trying to make his unbiblical teachings on self-esteem fit the Bible.

At the very end of *Hide or Seek* Dobson makes a another statement which is rather contradictory to the entire thrust of his book. He says, "May I stress, further, that the quest for self-esteem can take us in the direction of unacceptable pride."[38] Here is an entire book written for increasing self-esteem, and Dobson ends by saying that self-esteem can lead to ungodly pride. We thoroughly agree with Dobson here. It can certainly lead to pride. Not only is the possibility there. It is a very strong possibility. It could very well be that self-esteem will be the most iatrogenic "treatment" of all.

Based on what we say elsewhere in this volume, we contend that the quest for self-esteem very likely will and does "take us in the direction of unacceptable pride." Nevertheless, Dobson says:

> In summary, let me state what I hope has been obvious to this point. *Hide or Seek* does not reflect the philosophy of Me-ism. I have not suggested that children be taught arrogance and self-sufficiency or that they be lured into selfishness. (That will occur without any encouragement from parents.) My purpose has been to help mothers and fathers preserve an inner physical and mental and spiritual health. And I hope this final segment has taken us a few steps further in that direction.[39]

While *Hide or Seek* may not obviously "reflect the philosophy of Me-ism," Dobson's teachings do focus on the self. And while Dobson teaches against outright arrogance, there is a definite thrust toward self-sufficiency and a very probable result of subtle pride. Just as Maslow never intended that the hippie movement be the result of his self-actualization teachings and just as psychologists may not desire to sanction selfishness but do, so too, Dobson does not intend to have his self-esteem teachings end in pride, egoism or arrogance. However, the overwhelming tendency is definitely in that direction. Maslow eventually saw the shortcomings of his teachings.[40] Maybe Dobson will too.

Did Christ Teach a Healthy Self-Concept?

In order to make his self-esteem teachings seem biblical, Dobson says:

> The healthy self-concept which Christ taught, then, involves neither haughtiness and pride nor inferiority and worthlessness. It is one of humble reverence for God and every member of His human family.[41]

That sounds very good. However, that is not what Dobson is teaching throughout *Hide or Seek*. Only at the very end of the book does he bring in God and suggestions about teaching children to think about and esteem others.[42] It's kind of an afterthought to satisfy those who would question the self-centeredness of his self-esteem teachings.

Dobson's teachings in *Hide or Seek* did not originate from the Bible. They came from his involvement in secular psychology. If he had begun with the Bible he would not have picked up the *self-esteem* label with all of its secular humanistic underpinnings. Aside from those few statements about God and the Bible, there is little difference between what Dobson teaches about self-esteem and what godless secularists teach. While agreeing that the Bible teaches against pride, he is committed to feeding secular theories of the self to Christians.

Jesus taught truth, not what psychologists might call a "healthy self-concept." In response to Jesus' promise, "If ye continue in my word, then are ye my disciples indeed; and ye shall know the truth, and the truth shall make you free," some of his listeners objected. His words did not fit their "healthy self-concept."

They said, "We be Abraham's seed, and were never in bondage to any man: how sayest thou, Ye shall be made free?"

Jesus answered, "Whosoever committeth sin is the servant of sin." Then as the dialogue continued Jesus said to them: "Ye are of your father the devil, and the lusts of your father ye will do. . ." (John 8:31-34, 44). Was that a "healthy self-concept" or was it the truth?

Jesus emphasized relationship rather than self. For instance, in His final discourse with His disciples Jesus said:

> I am the vine, ye are the branches: He that abideth in me, and I in him, the same bringeth forth much fruit: for without me ye can do nothing. If a man abide not in me, he is cast forth as a branch, and is withered; and men gather them, and cast them into the fire, and they are burned. If ye abide in me, and my words abide in you, ye

shall ask what ye will, and it shall be done unto you. Herein is my Father glorified, that ye bear much fruit; so shall ye be my disciples. As the Father hath loved me, so have I loved you: continue ye in my love. If ye keep my commandments, ye shall abide in my love; even as I have kept my Father's commandments, and abide in His love (John 15:5-10).

While one might call this a "healthy self-concept," Jesus was emphasizing relationship and involvement, not selfhood. What a person does in relationship with Christ is what counts, not what he might think about himself or even who he is in himself. A person may think all kinds of wonderful thoughts about himself and not abide in Christ and thus be cast out as a withered branch. Notice the emphasis on obedience and fruitfulness rather than on who self is. While one might exclaim with wonder and awe, "I am in Christ!" the emphasis should be on "in Christ," not on "I am."

While believers have an identity in Christ, it is a relationship-concept rather than the kind of self-concept that would focus on who I am. Notice the relationship words which permeate Jesus' words to His disciples:

These things have I spoken unto you, that my joy might remain in you, and that your joy might be full. This is my commandment, That ye love one another, as I have loved you. Greater love hath no man than this, that a man lay down his life for his friends. Ye are my friends, if ye do whatsoever I command you. Henceforth I call you not servants; for the servant knoweth not what his lord doeth: but I have called you friends; for all things that I have heard of my Father I have made known unto you. Ye have not chosen me, but I have chosen you, and ordained you, that ye should go and bring forth fruit, and that your fruit should remain: that whatsoever ye shall ask of the Father in my name, he may give it you. These things I command you, that ye love one another. If the world hate you, ye know that it hated me before it hated you. If ye were of the world, the world would love his own: but because ye are not of the world, but I have chosen you out of the world, therefore the world hateth you (John 15:11-19).

There is a distinct difference between what the world of humanistic psychology has to offer and what Christ gives. Jesus chooses and loves those He has chosen. Their joy is to be found in Him, not in self. Their love emanates from His love for them. Thus, their love for one another does not come from self-love or self-esteem, nor does it enhance self-esteem. The emphasis is on relationship, fruit bearing, and preparing to be rejected by the world. Their identification is in Jesus to the point of suffering and following Him to the cross. Only through strained semantics, labored logic and exploited exegesis can one prove that self-esteem is biblical or even a part of the church tradition or teaching.

9

Loving Self

or

Denying Self?

A Commandment to Love Self?

Various teachers of self-esteem and self-love use the Great Commandment to justify self love.

> Thou shalt love the Lord thy God with all thy heart, and with all thy soul, and with all thy mind. This is the first and great commandment. And the second is like unto it, Thou shalt love thy neighbour as thyself. On these two commandments hang all the law and the prophets (Matthew 22:40).

Is the commandment to love self a commandment of God or is it a commandment of men?

Jesus accused the Pharisees of adding the commandments of men to the commandments of God (Matthew 15:9). Secular humanists and many Christians seek to prove that Jesus included a commandment to love self along with the commandment to love neighbor. If, indeed, the Bible commands us to love ourselves we must do so. However, if the Bible does **not** command us to love ourselves, then we have a modern counter-

151

part to the sect of the Pharisees: the sect of self-esteem psychologists.

In his Epilogue, added to the end of the revised version of *Hide or Seek*, Dobson says:

> Jesus commanded us to love our neighbors *as* ourselves, implying not only that we are permitted a reasonable expression of self-love, but that love for others is impossible—until we experience a measure of self-respect.[1] (Emphasis his.)

But, we found no Bible commentary that said that Matthew 22:39 (or parallel verses in Mark and Luke) means "that we are permitted a reasonable expression of self-love" or "that love for others is impossible until we experience a measure of self-respect." On the other hand, a couple of statements by humanistic psychologist Erich Fromm parallel the above statement by Dobson. Fromm says:

> If it is a virtue to love my neighbor as a human being, it must be a virtue—and not a vice—to love myself, since I am a human being too. There is no concept of man in which I myself am not included. A doctrine which proclaims such an exclusion proves itself to be intrinsically contradictory. The idea expressed in the Biblical "Love thy neighbor as thyself!" implies that respect for one's own integrity and uniqueness, love for and understanding of one's own self, can not be separated from respect for and love and understanding of another individual. The love for my own self is inseparably connected with the love for any other self.[2]

> If an individual is able to love productively, he loves himself too; if he can love *only* others, he can not love at all."[3] (Emphasis his.)

Fromm was an atheist who argued against the fundamentals of the Christian faith. Dobson's understanding of Jesus' words about loving neighbor as one loves himself is similar to that of Fromm and other psychological theorists. Rather than properly exegeting the passage, those people use Scripture to support a pet theory.

Dobson's Epilogue at the end of *Hide or Seek* not only falls short of its intent, but also reveals errors in his thinking and theology. Dobson may protest that he speaks out against pride in this same section. However, even here there is confusion. He says:

> Then what *is* the biblical meaning of pride? I believe sinful pride occurs when our arrogant self-sufficiency leads us to violate the two most basic commandments of Jesus: first, to love God with all our heart, mind and strength; and second, to love our neighbor as ourselves.[4] (Emphasis his.)

The confusion is that Dobson has already declared that the Second Commandment means "not only that we are permitted a reasonable expression of self-love, but that love for others is impossible—until we experience a measure of self-respect."[5] And, since it does not mean what Dobson says it does, no amount of amplification of the Second Commandment will rescue his attempt to make it condone and command self-love. Even truth added to error will not result in truth.

In a Focus on the Family interview, marriage and family counselor H. Norman Wright declares: "You can't be happily married to another person unless you're happily married to yourself." Dobson answers, "There's a scriptural basis for that—to love others as you love yourself."[6] Christians who teach self-love regularly quote Matthew 22:40 and Mark 12:30 in defense of loving self. But Jesus was not talking about loving oneself emotionally. He used the word *agapao* when He said:

Thou shalt love the Lord thy God with all thy heart, and
with all thy soul, and with all thy mind. This is the first
and great commandment. And the second is like unto it,
Thou shalt love thy neighbour as thyself. On these two
commandments hang all the law and the prophets
(Matthew 22:40).

Agapao is volitional love, not the emotional love of affection
or liking or feeling good about someone. It has to do with will
and action. Thus love for God is expressed in trust, obedience,
commitment, and service. Love for neighbor would be doing
good for that person. *Vine's Dictionary of New Testament Words*
explains it this way:

Christian love, whether exercised toward the brethren, or
toward men generally, is not an impulse from feelings, it
does not always run with the natural inclinations, nor
does it spend itself only upon those for whom an affinity
is discovered. Love seeks the welfare of all, Rom. 15:2,
and works no ill to any, 13:8-10; love seeks opportunity to
do good to "all men, and especially toward them that are
of the household of the faith," Gal . 6:10.[7]

The concept of self-love is not the subject of the Great
Commandment. It is only a qualifier. When Jesus commands
people to love God with "all thy heart, and with all thy soul,
and with all thy mind, and with all thy strength" (Mark 12:30),
He is emphasizing the all-encompassing nature of this love
(beyond the possibility of the natural man and only possible
through divine grace). If He had used the same words for loving
neighbor, He would have encouraged idolatry. However, for the
next degree of intensity he used the words *as thyself.*

Jesus does **not** command people to love themselves. He
does not say there are three commandments (love God, love
neighbor, and love self). Instead, he says, "On these **two**
commandments hang all the law and the prophets" (Matthew
22:40). **Love of self is a fact, not a command**. In fact, Jesus

would not command people to love others as themselves if they do not already love themselves. It would be a pointless statement. Furthermore, if self-love were a necessity for loving others, it would have to precede love for God and love for others. To fit self-love theology, the first commandment would have to read: "Love yourself first so that you will be able to love God and others."

Scripture teaches that people **do** love themselves. Paul says, "For no man ever yet hated his own flesh; but nourisheth and cherisheth it, even as the Lord the church" (Ephesians 5:29). Some biblical references to people loathing themselves have to do with knowing that their deeds are evil (e. g., Ezekiel 36:31). In those instances they are still committed to themselves and retain biases that are favorable to themselves until they turn to the Lord and confess their sin.

Often those who complain about not loving themselves are dissatisfied with their lives—their feelings, abilities, circumstances, and behavior. If they truly hated themselves they would be happy to be miserable. All human beings love themselves even when they are not **feeling** fond of themselves.

From the totality of Scripture, the love one naturally has toward self is commanded to be directed toward others. We are not commanded to love self. We already do. We are commanded to love others as much as we already love ourselves. The story of the Good Samaritan, which follows the commandment to love one's neighbor, illustrates not only who is our neighbor, but what is meant by the word *love*. Here love means to extend oneself beyond the point of convenience to accomplish what is deemed best for the neighbor. The idea is that we should seek the good of others just as fully as we seek good (or what we may want or even mistakenly think is good) for ourselves—just as naturally as we tend to care for our own personal well-being.

Another Scripture that parallels this same idea of loving others as we already do ourselves is Luke 6:31-35, which begins with: "And as ye would that men should do to you, do ye also to them likewise." Evidently Jesus assumed that His listeners wanted to be treated justly, kindly, and mercifully. In other words, they wanted to be treated according to expressions of love rather than expressions of indifference or animosity.

The kind of love that Jesus emphasized is that which is selfless and not motivated by gaining returns. He says, "But love ye your enemies. . . . For if ye love them which love you, what thank have ye? for sinners also love those that love them." (Luke 6:27,32). Since it is natural for people to attend to their own needs and desires, Jesus turned their attention beyond themselves.

Biblical love for others comes **first** from God's love and then by responding in wholehearted love for Him (with all of one's heart, soul, mind and strength). And, one cannot do that unless he knows Him and is infused with His love and life. The Scripture says, "We love Him because He first loved us" (1 John 4:19). A person cannot truly love (*agapao*) God without first knowing His love by grace; and one cannot truly love neighbor as self without first loving God. The proper biblical position for a Christian is not to encourage, justify, or establish self-love, but rather to devote one's life to loving God and loving neighbor as self. Jay Adams explains it this way:

> There is no need for concern about how to love one's self, for so long as one seeks first to love God and his neighbor in a biblical fashion, all proper self-concern will appear as a by-product. That is why the Bible never commands us to love ourselves. Since the Bible is silent on the matter, we should be too.[8]

Loving Self or Denying Self?

If the Bible does not teach us to love ourselves, what does it say to do about ourselves? Dobson fears that if people do not love and esteem themselves they will wallow in the depths of low self-esteem and self-hatred. He repeatedly describes such poor souls and says that if something isn't done to help them love themselves their lives will end in disaster. Yet the Bible does not present that message.

The Bible reveals that self is the problem and the cross is the answer. K. P. Yohannan, in his book *Road to Reality,* says:

> The cross has two operations. First, on it Christ paid the penalty for our sins and thus bought our eternal salvation. But it doesn't stop there. The second work of the cross provides for our ongoing sanctification—the daily, continuous crucifixion of our flesh. This great doctrine is not very popular lately because it requires a voluntary acceptance of death to ego or self. . . . This is why Paul says in 2 Corinthians 4:10 that we are "always bearing about in the body the dying of the Lord Jesus, that the life also of Jesus might be made manifest in our body." Accepting death to my ego is the only way to manifest the life of Christ. Putting my "self" to death is the only way to exchange my life for His.[9]

The first and foremost cross is, of course, the cross of Christ. However, Jesus says that there is a second cross for dealing with the self and its demands.

> Then said Jesus unto his disciples, If any man will come after me, let him deny himself, and take up his cross, and follow me. For whosoever will save his life shall lose it: and whosoever will lose his life for my sake shall find it. For what is a man profited, if he shall gain the whole world, and lose his own soul? Or what shall a man give in exchange for his soul? For the Son of man shall come in the glory of his Father with his angels; and then he shall reward every man according to his works (Matthew 16:24-27).

Following Jesus thus entails denying self and taking up one's cross.

What does it mean to deny self, take up the cross, and follow Christ? Jay Adams answers these questions in his excellent book *The Biblical View of Self-Esteem, Self-Love, Self-Image*. He says:

> The words translated "self" and "life" (*heauton* and *psuche*) both mean "self" and refer to the same thing. . . . Christ is telling us not only to say no to ourselves and yes to Him ("follow me"), but He affirms that we must put self to death by "taking up our cross" (Luke adds "daily"). To take up the cross does not mean making some particular sacrifice, nor does it refer to some particular burden ("My husband is my cross"). Anyone in that day, reading those words, would know plainly that taking up the cross meant one and only one thing: putting to death an infamous criminal. Jesus, therefore, is saying, "You must treat yourself, with all your sinful ways, priorities, and desires, like a criminal, and put self to death every day." That says something about the self-image that Christ expects us to have![10]

Denying oneself involves losing one's life for Christ's sake. While this includes the possibility of literally dying for one's faith in Christ, it also means dying to all of the old ways of the self. And this must include denying oneself the self-teachings of secular humanists, who only know what it is to live after the flesh. In fact, psychological teachings, influenced by the theories of non-Christians, are limited to living after the flesh, which is to be put off by Christians.

Self-esteem, self-love, and self-worth are attitudes from the altars of Fromm, Adler, Maslow, and Rogers and are included in the ways of the self that are to be denied and crucified, even if such concepts are reworked and restated by Christians.

In John 12:25 Jesus says, "He that loveth his life shall lose it; and he that hateth his life in this world shall keep it unto life eternal." This is a strong warning against the promotion of self-love even though the word *hateth* in this context means "to love less" in the same way that the word is used in Luke 14:26, which says:

> If any man come to me, and hate not his father, and mother, and wife, and children, and brethren, and sisters, yea, and his own life also, he cannot be my disciple. And whosoever doth not bear his cross, and come after me, cannot be my disciple (Luke 14:26-27).

Adams warns:

> The consequences of self-love dogma are very serious. These words of Jesus warn of eternal deprivation. One wonders how many young people will be led astray, led away from discipleship for Christ, which requires losing their "selves," because they were told "Feel good about yourself" rather than being told that there is a criminal inside who needs to be put to death daily.[11]

Might the pathetic examples of young people suffering from low self-esteem and a lack of self-love, so graphically illustrated by Dobson, find their lives in this world through increasing self-esteem, but lose their own souls? In trying "to help parents protect their children from the epidemic of self-hatred that has besieged an entire generation of young people,"[12] could Dobson be wrong in his diagnosis and remedy? If so, there could be eternal consequences.

Yohannan says:

> Today we have substituted a religion of good vibes and trouble-free living for the commands of the Master. He said, "Take up your cross and follow Me," but we have clenched our fists and refused to open our palms. We won't receive the nail because it would mean death to our "self." We demand instead to pleasure our desires for self-gratification. And we have found shepherds and Bible

teachers who will give us a "feel good" theology to match and justify our lives of sinful rebellion.[13]

He also says this about what it means to follow Jesus:

It is obvious that Jesus will have no one among His followers who is wanting to put comfort, family ties or security in this world ahead of His kingdom. Jesus is saying [in Luke 9:57-62], in effect, "I offer you what I have—hardship, hunger, labor, loneliness, rejection, sweat, tears and death. I'm a stranger and pilgrim in this world, and if you follow Me you'll have to break away from the clinging attachments of this present life."[14]

The battle between the flesh (the ways of the old self) and the Spirit (living in the believer) is ongoing and cannot be ignored. Self is always ready to assume center stage even in the lives of dedicated Christians. That is why the self-teachings from secularists, who are still living under the influence of Satan (Ephesians 2:2), are so dangerous. And that is why Christians must daily deny themselves, take up their cross, and follow Jesus. They must diligently put off the old self and put on the new. What must constantly be denied is the old authority of self ruling the life, of self having its own way, and of self living in such a way as to please itself. It boils down to putting God's will and interests before one's own.

Denying self, rather than esteeming self, equips people to say "No" to sin when they are indwelt by the Holy Spirit. Instead of esteem, following Jesus and thereby denying the self is the biblical antidote to illegal drugs and illicit sex. Self-control, not self-love, is a fruit of the Spirit.

Dobson's line of thinking seems to be that building self-esteem will keep kids from taking drugs, which will then allow them to develop self-control. Dr. Robert Smith illustrates that kind of faulty reasoning. He says:

Actually, Dobson's whole philosophy is reversed by the very first statement in this chapter [6 of *Dare to Discipline*]: "There is no more certain destroyer of self-discipline and self-control than the abusive use of drugs." (190) The difficulty is that he has it backwards. The use of drugs results from lack of biblical self-control and self-discipline rather than the other way around.[15]

Self-control, not self-esteem, is God's remedy through His active presence in the life of a believer. God calls and enables Christians to crucify the flesh and its passions rather than to increase self-esteem and self-love.

The Danger of Self-Love

While Dobson and others encourage self-esteem, self-worth, self-acceptance and thereby self-love, the Bible warns about the danger of having a fondness for oneself, of cherishing the self. Paul says:

> This know, also, that in the last days perilous times shall come. For men shall be lovers of their own selves, covetous, boasters, proud, blasphemers, disobedient to parents, unthankful, unholy, without natural affection, trucebreakers, false accusers, incontinent, fierce, despisers of those that are good, traitors, heady, highminded, lovers of pleasures more than lovers of God, having a form of godliness, but denying the power thereof; from such turn away (2 Timothy 3:1-5).

Notice the list of adjectives that describe "lovers of their own selves." They certainly match up with the current increase in illicit entertainment, materialism, teenage rebellion, fornication, rape, adultery, divorce, drunkenness, hatred of God, and other forms of pleasure-seeking self-centeredness.

This prophecy is being at least partly fulfilled today. The escalation in self-centered, self-pleasing crimes has risen dramatically. When one looks at the increasing emphasis on self-love, self-esteem, self-acceptance, and self-seeking, one can see the disastrous results of selfishness going rampant. Psychologists present self-esteem and self-love as the remedy for illegal drugs and illicit sex. But, those social problems have increased proportionately to the increase in self-esteem and self-love teachings. At least one study links high self-esteem with heavy involvement with drugs.[16]

When such crimes are viewed from a biblical perspective, one can see that selfishness (loving self more than loving God or others) is at the center. But when they are viewed from a humanistic, psychological perspective, the reason is low self-esteem. For instance, Dobson relates rape and homicide to low self-esteem,[17] but one cannot help but think that rape and murder are very selfish acts (loving pleasure and having one's way more than loving God). And Dobson sees low self-esteem at the bottom of illegal drug use. Yet using illegal drugs is loving pleasure more than loving God.

Paul says that lovers of themselves are covetous, not satisfied with what they have. Covetousness can include wanting more abilities, more significance, more love, more attention, more material possessions, and more pleasure. Covetousness does not disappear by acquiring more. The more covetousness gets, the more it wants. It becomes more lustful so that normal means of finding pleasure no longer satisfy. Thus, covetousness leads to indulging in pornography and sexual perversion. Dobson has been a fine champion against pornography while at the same time advocating self-love which, according to 2 Timothy 3:1, can easily move in that direction.

Boasting, another description of self-love, has also increased during the past few decades. The Bible says:

> Let another man praise thee, and not thine own mouth; a stranger, and not thine own lips (Proverbs 27:2).

Even among Christians, there is boasting. If one does not praise himself on a job resumé or during a job interview he is not likely to be hired these days. And while pride always seems to lurk in the depths of the soul, it is much more acceptable now than just a few decades ago. Richard Baxter of the seventeenth century wrote: "A proud mind is high in conceit, self-esteem, and carnal aspiring; a humble mind is high indeed in God's esteem, and in holy aspiring."[18] We commend Dobson for speaking out against boasting and pride, but his teachings on self-esteem and self-love often lead his followers in that very direction.

Dobson sees a vast difference between egotistical pride and a sense of self-love, self-worth, and self-esteem. While there are degrees of pride as expressed in boasting and haughtiness, the difference may sometimes depend on how much visible evidence surfaces from the depths of pride. Often pride is difficult to detect because it hides behind hurts and false humility. Pride leads to unforgiveness, resentment, bitterness, revenge, and many other outward expressions of sin. Pride is one of the most insidious, self-deceptive forms of sin which lurks in the flesh, always ready to defend, justify, exonerate, and glorify the self. That is why the thrust of the Bible is upward to God and outward to each other, rather than inward to the self. In contrast, the self-esteem movement is fertile soil for the inborn roots of pride to flourish.

Although Dobson says many good things about helping parents deal with rebellion in their children, such as being consistent and caring, he nevertheless may be adding fuel to that rebellion by promoting self-esteem and self-love. Christian parents, who in all earnestness desire the very best for their children, may be turning their children into lovers of self rather than lovers of God, under the influence of self-esteem promises and programs.

Paul describes "lovers of their own selves" as "unthankful, unholy," and "without natural affection." This seems to echo the first chapter of his letter to the Romans.

> Because that, when they knew God, they glorified him
> not as God, neither were thankful; but became vain in
> their imaginations, and their foolish heart was darkened.
> Professing themselves to be wise, they became fools. . . .
> Who changed the truth of God into a lie, and worshiped
> and served the creature more than the Creator, who is
> blessed for ever. Amen. For this cause God gave them up
> unto vile affections: for even their women did change the
> natural use into that which is against nature: And like-
> wise also the men, leaving the natural use of the woman,
> burned in their lust one toward another; men with men
> working that which is unseemly, and receiving in them-
> selves that recompence of their error which was meet
> (Romans 1:21-22, 25-27).

Notice how not glorifying God and being unthankful leads
to relying on human wisdom, self-worship (a form of self-love)
and then into unnatural affection. Rather than God being
honored and thanked, self is honored and acknowledged as
wise. Could those self-love teachings of humanistic psychology
be at least partly responsible for anti-family aspects of the
women's liberation movement and for the rise in homosexuality? If so, the "foremost advocate of the family," by promoting
some of the same self-teachings, may inadvertently be working
against the family.

Perhaps one of the most devastating descriptions of "lovers
of their own selves" and "lovers of pleasures more than lovers of
God" is their "having a form of godliness but denying the power
thereof." That is exactly what Christians are doing when they
turn to psychology to understand the human condition and to
remedy the problems of living. Instead of having confidence in
the sufficiency of the Word of God and the work of the Holy
Spirit, they are "denying the power" of Christ working in and
through them.

In looking to such men as Freud, Skinner, Adler, Maslow,
and Rogers, they become "heady, highminded" in their knowledge of psychology. But worse than that, they encourage others

to drink from the cistern of men's minds rather than from the pure water of the Word. There is something distinctly "unholy" about adding self-esteem and self-love to the teachings of Jesus. That is why Paul warns: "From such turn away."

Biblical Alternative to Self-Love

Rather than being a sanction to love self, the Great Commandment is the biblical alternative to self-love. The focus of love in the Bible is upward and outward instead of inward. Love is both an attitude and action to one another. And while love may include sentiment and emotional affection, it is primarily volitional action for the glory of God and the good of others. Thus when Jesus said, "Thou shalt love the Lord thy God with all thy heart, and with all thy soul, and with all thy mind, and with all thy strength" (Mark 12:30), He was saying that all of our being is to be committed to loving and, therefore, pleasing God. Love for God is expressed in a thankful heart committed to doing what pleases God according to what has been revealed in the Bible. It is not a grudging kind of obedience, but an eagerness to conform to His gracious will and to agree with God that He is the standard for all that is right and good.

The Second commandment is an extension or expression of the First Commandment: "Thou shalt love thy neighbor as thyself" (Mark 12:31). John elaborates on this. He describes the sequence of love. In contrast to the teachers of self-love, who say that people cannot love God and others until they love themselves, John says that love originates with God and then extends to others:

> We love Him because He first loved us. If a man say, I love God, and hateth his brother, he is a liar: for he that loveth not his brother whom he hath seen, how can he love God whom he hath not seen? And this command-

ment have we from Him, that he who loveth God love his brother also (1 John 4:19-21).

He loved us first, which enables us to love God, which then expresses itself in love for one another. In fact, according to John the prerequisite for authentic love (nonself-serving love) is being born of God and knowing God. He says.

Beloved, let us love one another: for love is of God; and every one that loveth is born of God, and knoweth God. He that loveth not knoweth not God; for God is love (I John 4:7,8).

While Fromm, Maslow, Rogers and others, who have rejected God's love through the sacrifice of His Son, may write volumes about love, they are insensitive to the kind of love that comes from God and motivates a person to truly love God and others. They may have feelings that they call love and human affection, but they are limited to a love which originates from the sinful nature inherited from Adam's fall. That is the very love they promote. It is self-love. Love for self motivates one to follow his own agenda, to ventilate feelings, to be "understood," to justify self and to blame someone or something else. Godly love for others motivates Christians to put God's interests above their own. Godly love includes confessing sin and repenting, both of which can be very painful and devastating to the ego.

The love of God is just the opposite of self-love or self-serving love. It is sacrificial love as expressed by Christ on the cross.

Herein is love, not that we loved God, but that he loved us, and sent his Son to be the propitiation for our sins. Beloved, if God so loved us, we ought also to love one another (1 John 4:10-11).

Jesus said:

This is my commandment, That ye love one another, as I have loved you. Greater love hath no man than this, that a man lay down his life for his friends (John 15:12-13).

Paul reminds us:

For when we were yet without strength, in due time Christ died for the ungodly. . . . But God commendeth his love toward us, in that, while we were yet sinners, Christ died for us (Romans 5:6, 8).

The Bible is about giving love, about sacrificial love. It neither teaches nor encourages self-serving love or self-esteem. Many of Dobson's suggestions about disciplining in love, listening to our children, showing them kindness and respect, and being consistent are excellent suggestions. The Bible already teaches us to do those things—to discipline our children with consistency, fairness, and love. The Bible already teaches us to love one another (even our enemies) in word and deed, in kindness and in service. The Bible teaches us to esteem one another so that our children will learn to esteem and respect one another as well. Moreover, it is Christ in us who enables us to follow His Word. The presence of His life in the believer works together with the written Word of God. A number of biblical instructions for love and discipline are similar to those encouraged by Dobson. But the biblical goal is to teach children to love God and one another by Jesus' life and His Word, rather than to build self-esteem.

From Adam's first breath, mankind was designed to live in relationship with God, not as an autonomous self. The entire Bible rests on that relationship, for after Jesus answered the Pharisee by saying that the Greatest Commandment is to love God and the second is to love neighbor as oneself, He said: "On these two commandments hang all the law and the prophets" (Matthew 22:40). Jesus came to save us from self and to reestablish that love relationship for which we were created. Through the centuries books have been written about loving

God and loving one another. However, in recent decades the church has been inundated with books telling us how to love ourselves better, esteem ourselves more, accept ourselves no matter what, and build our own self-worth.

10

Truth
or
Self-Deception?

Where is all of this self-esteem leading us? Is all of this self-esteem talk a blessing or a bane to God's people? Are Dobson and the other professing Christian self-esteem teachers leading us down a primrose path? This pseudo-biblical, pseudo-scientific self-esteem surge in the church is one of its biggest potential curses. It began as a little leaven, but like a little leaven it has permeated the entire loaf. There is hardly a place in the church where self-esteem teachings are not found and accepted as an antidote to life's problems, or at least as an adjunct to the Bible. We shall show how the self-esteem leaven turned loose has the potential to lead many away from the eternal truths of God.

The little leaven begins with the idea that everyone experiences low self-esteem and that everyone needs a certain degree of self-esteem in order to be successful and productive. The formula is simple enough: low self-esteem equates to low success and high self-esteem leads to high success. The reasoning follows that those who are failures in life are the ones with low self-esteem. It does not matter if one is involved in one or more of the six social problem areas studied by the Task Force (mentioned earlier) or if one is simply experiencing a degree of failure in one or more areas of life. The answer is to raise self-esteem and prestissimo! Failure turns to success and irresponsible people become responsible. Social problems disappear and the world becomes a better place to live in. . . or so the leaders of this litany would have us believe, in spite of the lack of a biblical base or research support.

Dr. Nathaniel Branden, popular writer and speaker, and best-known secular self-esteem psychologist sounds like Dobson when he says:

> Tell me how a person judges his or her self-esteem and I will tell you how that person operates at work, in love, in sex, in parenting, in every important aspect of existence, and how high he or she is likely to rise. The reputation you have within yourself, your self-esteem, is the single most important factor for a fulfilling life.[1]

If low self-esteem were labeled a disease, it would be the most prevalent disease in America according to the way many view it. However, the truth is that man is not plagued with low self-esteem.

Someone might say, "I know people who hate themselves. How would you explain that?" People do say this. However, is this how they truly feel or is this a way of drawing sympathy and support from others? If they tell someone they hate themselves, the common response is to rescue them from that idea. In the process they receive sympathy and support not normally given. It is a predictable transaction that once begun can become a habitual way of relating to others and receiving support. On the other hand, there are some who do experience a personal revulsion because of their sin. In that case, they need to confess and repent and be cleansed, not told to love themselves more.

Now we are not saying that there are no individuals who genuinely think that they hate themselves. However, what they generally hate is something about themselves or their circumstances. They exhibit actual love for themselves in that they continue to spend most of their time concerned about themselves, even if it is with unhappy thoughts. They generally get to the point where they are unhappy about themselves because a discrepancy exists between their aspirations or desires and their performance or condition. This intensive hate is evidence of high self-interest. As an example of this, *Women's Health and Fitness News* reports:

> In one [study] in 1987, nearly 9,000 women admitted that they are not at all happy with what their mirrors reflect: 12% said they are extremely dissatisfied, 16% are quite dissatisfied and 25% are somewhat dissatisfied. The women are most discontent with their thighs, hips, buttocks, stomachs and waists. In another survey of 33,000 women in 1986, 75% thought they were too fat and 64% were unhappy with their stomachs, 61% with their hips, and 72% with their thighs. Only 1% were totally happy with their bodies.[2]

Thus a woman who aspires to look like Jane Fonda, but is actually fat and ugly by cultural standards, could end up hating her condition and thereby think that she hates herself because her desire to look like Jane Fonda is discrepant from the reality of being fat and "ugly." She is reacting to the discrepancy. It is the aspiration-actuality-discrepancy that is the root of the problem. She does not really hate herself. She hates the discrepancy. If she truly hated herself she would be happy, or at least satisfied, to be fat and ugly. But, her self-love in tandem with the discrepancy makes her miserable. Now Dobson does touch on this idea, but more as an afterthought or as an exception rather than the rule.[3] And this is one great weakness of Dobson in that he takes exceptions, such as low self-esteem, and makes them the rule; and he takes the rules (i.e. resilience of children) and makes them the exception.

Dr. David Myers, in his book *The Inflated Self*, discusses the research having to do with how we view ourselves and others. The research demonstrates that there is definitely a self-serving bias at work in individuals. Myers says:

> Time and again, experiments have revealed that people tend to attribute positive behaviors to themselves and negative behaviors to external factors, enabling them to take credit for their good acts and to deny responsibility for their bad acts.[4]

A plethora of research studies contradict the common notion of the self-esteemers having to do with self-image. In his book Myers presents research to support his statement that:

> Preachers who deliver ego-boosting pep talks to audiences who are supposedly plagued with miserable self-images are preaching to a problem that seldom exists.[5]

Another book, coauthored by Myers and Malcolm Jeeves, states that "the most common error in people's self images is not unrealistically low self-esteem, but rather self-serving pride; not an inferiority complex, but a superiority complex."[6]

A recent study conducted by Scott Allison *et al.* indicates that people give themselves reasons to think positively about themselves. For instance, they regard themselves more highly than others by remembering unfair actions against themselves instead of their own unfairness to others.[7]

There is a definite self-serving bias in all of us. Self-esteem and self-love do not need to be encouraged; they are part of the fallen, sinful nature. In Jeremiah 17:9 we are told, "The heart is deceitful above all things and desperately wicked." Man is self-serving, self-affirming, self-loving, and self-esteeming because he is self-deceiving. Many of the ways that man serves, affirms, loves, esteems, and deceives himself are found in the research as well as the Bible.

Positive Illusions: Creative Self-Deception and the Healthy Mind

The issue at stake is truth. Truth is extremely important to God. So much so that Jesus promised to send the Spirit of Truth to indwell His disciples. Conversely, Satan is a deceiver and the father of lies. How much self-deception is involved in the process of developing high self-esteem?

Dr. Shelley Taylor and Dr. Jonathon Brown, in an article titled "Illusion and Well-Being: A Social Psychological Perspective on Mental Health," propose that "accurate self-knowledge may be negatively related to psychological health."[8] In other words, they are suggesting that "positive illusion" (self-deception) may be good for a person. They discuss research that challenges the traditional view of mental health. In a summary they say:

> Many prominent theorists have argued that accurate perceptions of the self, the world, and the future are essential for mental health. Yet considerable research evidence suggests that overly positive self-evaluations, exaggerated perceptions of control or mastery, and unrealistic optimism are characteristic of normal human thought. . . . These strategies may succeed, in large part, because both the social world and cognitive-processing mechanisms impose filters on incoming information that distort it in a positive direction; negative information may be isolated and represented in as unthreatening a manner as possible.[9]

Taylor discusses these same findings in her book *Positive Illusions: Creative Self-Deception and the Healthy Mind.*[10] Numerous authors are quoted by Taylor and Brown to demonstrate that "the view that psychological health depends on accurate perceptions of reality has been widely promulgated and widely shared in the literature on mental health."[11] To challenge this view, Taylor and Brown discuss the extensive research on illusions. They distinguish illusion from error and bias as follows:

> *Error* and *bias* imply short-term mistakes and distortions, respectively, that might be caused by careless oversight or other temporary negligences. *Illusion*, in contrast, implies a more general, enduring pattern of error, bias, or both that assumes a particular direction or shape.[12]

They use the following definition of *illusion*:

> . . . a perception that represents what is perceived in a way different from the way it is in reality. An illusion is a false mental image or conception which may be a misinterpretation of a real appearance or may be something imagined. It may be pleasing, harmless, or even useful.[13]

In summary they say that the research:

> . . . documents that normal individuals possess unrealistically positive views of themselves, an exaggerated belief in their ability to control their environment, and a view of the future that maintains that their future will be far better than the average person's.[14]

Taylor and Brown comment about the individual's unrealistically positive view of self, exaggerated belief in their ability to control their environment, and an optimistic view of the future:

Unrealistically Positive Views of the Self:

> Suggestive evidence indicates that individuals who are low in self-esteem, moderately depressed, or both are more balanced in self-perceptions.[15]

Illusions of Control:

Realistic perceptions of personal control thus appear to be more characteristic of individuals in a depressed affective state than individuals in an undepressed affective state.[16]

Unrealistic Optimism:

In contrast to the extremely positive view of the future displayed by normal individuals, moderately depressed people and those with low self-esteem appear to entertain more balanced assessments of their likely future circumstances.[17]

We would like to suggest that in all of the above cases that "are more balanced in self-perceptions," have "realistic perceptions of personal control," and have "balanced assessments of their likely future circumstances" are moderately depressed for those very reasons. On the other hand, Taylor and Brown say:

The mentally healthy person appears to have the enviable capacity to distort reality in a direction that enhances self-esteem, maintains beliefs in personal efficacy, and promotes an optimistic view of the future.[18] (Emphasis added.)

The contrast between the "mentally healthy person" and the depressed individual is used to suggest that individuals should be encouraged to establish or sustain positive illusions in order to enhance their self-esteem and thereby to be successful. Taylor and Brown say:

The individual who responds to negative, ambiguous, or unsupportive feedback with a positive sense of self, a belief in personal efficacy, and an optimistic sense of the future will, we maintain, be happier, more caring, and more productive than the individual who perceives this same information accurately and integrates it into his or her view of the self, the world, and the future. In this sense, the capacity to develop and maintain positive illusions may be thought of as a valuable human resource to be nurtured and promoted, rather than an error-prone processing system to be corrected.[19]

The self-esteem, self-love industry is based on people's willingness and even desire to be deceived. After all, if one wants to feel good about himself and has not enough supportive evidence in his life for that, he will probably try to supply the evidence through blaming others for his misfortune, attempting to excel in some way to be at least as good as or better than others, or deceiving himself into thinking that he is better than he is. In fact, the apparent purpose of Taylor's book *Positive Illusions* is to justify and promote self-deception because she seems to believe that self-esteem is more important than truth. That is diametrically opposed to Jesus' words, "Ye shall know the truth, and the truth shall make you free" (John 8:32).

We think that individuals who continue to sustain their illusions in order to enhance or maintain their self-esteem, personal control, and optimism about the future are extremely unlikely to sense a need for God or His Son. If the positive illusionists cannot or will not face the truth about themselves, it is unlikely that they will face the truth about their deceitful hearts and thus they will be most unlikely to see a need for God.

Such individuals are hiding beneath their positive illusions and will generally see no need for a Savior. Why should they? Exaggerated positive illusions that sustain self-esteem, a false sense of personal control and an unrealistic optimism about the future leave little room for the cross. That was the Pharisees' problem. As Jesus said, only those who think they are sick go to the physician. Professing Christians who continue in their creative self-deceptions are less likely to walk with Him.

There are those who think that it is necessary to have good self-esteem to be able to believe that God loves them. But that reveals a kind of theology that puts the reason for God's love in the person being lovable or having some goodness, rather than in the greatness of God's mercy, love, and grace. On the other hand, those who "are more balanced in self-perceptions," have "realistic perceptions of personal control" and "balanced assessments of their future circumstances," and are depressed as a result do seem ripe for the Gospel. By revealing truth, the Holy Spirit convicts of sin and manifests Christ. He does not bring sinners to faith through self-deception!

Those individuals who know Christ as Savior but continue to be depressed are in need of sound biblical teaching about God's love, not unsound secular teaching about self-esteem. When they truly know self, circumstances and the future there may be much to be depressed about. But, when they come to believe God sent His Son to cover this ugly reality, there is reason to rejoice. A person who lives under self-deceptive illusions may have a greater opportunity for worldly success, but he is a less likely candidate for God's dear Son or the initial and continuing work of the Holy Spirit.

Some of Dobson's main emotional appeals are his vivid descriptions of children with low self-esteem. Dobson says, "I think you would be wise folks to start talking about inferiority with your three-year-old."[20] He also says, "A little child is born with an irrepressible inclination to question his own worth."[21] Dobson believes that people may not remember when their self-doubt began because it "originated during your earliest days of conscious existence."[22] He contends that from that early inborn self-doubt, "It is not uncommon for a pre-kindergartener to have concluded already that he is terribly ugly, incredibly dumb, unloved, unneeded, foolish or strange."[23] Then he says, "These early feelings of inadequacy. . . lurk just below the conscious mind and are never far from awareness."[24]

Once more Dobson is wrong. His conclusions about low self-esteem in children have no biblical support and are contradicted by the research. Taylor, in her book *Positive Illusions*, gives much research to support the idea that positive illusions and self-esteem begin early in life and may be part of the fabric of being human. She says:

Mild positive illusions appear to be characteristic of the majority of people under a broad array of circumstances. . . . The evidence from studies with children suggests that positive illusions may actually be wired in, inherent in how the mind processes and ascribes meaning to information. The fact that positive illusions are typically so much stronger in children than in adults argues against the idea that they are learned adaptations to life.[25]

Taylor is not concerned about raising young children's self-esteem by using positive illusions, because they are already adept at that. She says that while people may learn more complex ways of deceiving themselves, such self-deception is not a learned behavior:

Rather, the basic form of positive illusions—seeing the self, one's potency, and the future in a falsely positive manner—may not have to be learned. In fact, the opposite appears to be true. Positive illusions may actually have to be unlearned, at least to a degree, for people to function effectively in the adult world.[26]

In other words, children naturally have high self-esteem through positive illusions. The self-esteem teachings of Dobson contradict the revelations about positive illusions and self-deception, although self-delusions do require constant reinforcement from others, from self, from possessions or attributes, or from achievement and success.

Self-Esteem and Self Righteousness

Dobson does not make a clear distinction between how Christians and non-Christians live. Instead he is interested in promoting a Judeo-Christian ethic—something often different from biblical Christianity.[27] There is a distinct difference in the very nature of one who has been born of the Spirit and one who has not. Additionally, even after a person has been saved by grace he encounters the ongoing battle between the flesh and the Spirit (Galatians 5). One cannot please God in the flesh by trying to follow an ethic which only resembles Christianity. True Christianity can be lived only by the power of the Holy Spirit indwelling the believer.

No human activity or self-improvement system can change the heart. No human system of ethics or psychological change can do what only the Spirit of God can do in a person, not only at the point of new birth but throughout the process of sanctification. This is true for children as well as adults. However, self-esteem has become the currency of American cultural success. Its insidious nature zooms the focus in on me, myself and I—and on what I can do and even on what a good person I am. It may be sustained by self-deception or repeated success or an attitude of self-righteousness—a sense of one's own goodness.

Jesus tells the story of two men:

> Two men went up into the temple to pray; the one a Pharisee, and the other a publican. The Pharisee stood and prayed thus with himself, God, I thank thee, that I am not as other men are, extortioners, unjust, adulterers, or even as this publican. I fast twice in the week, I give tithes of all that I possess. And the publican, standing afar off, would not lift up so much as his eyes unto heaven, but smote upon his breast saying, God be merciful to me a sinner. I tell you, this man went down to his house justified rather than the other: for every one that exalteth himself shall be abased; and he that humbleth himself shall be exalted (Luke: 18:10-14).

Which man exhibited high self-esteem? If Jesus had wanted to teach the importance of self-esteem He would have ended this parable differently. He would have sent the poor publican to a local psychologist to build his self-esteem.

Self-esteem, self-love, and self-worth fit very well into American middle-class morality. American citizens can feel good about themselves, especially if they follow a so-called Judeo-Christian ethic. But, Christians need to take a more accurate, biblical view of ourselves, a more humble view, and recognize that "all our righteousnesses [apart from Christ] are as filthy rags" (Isaiah 64:6). And while God has greatly blessed us, we have not always reflected His goodness and grace but have put on self-righteousness. Self-esteem and self-righteousness go hand in hand.

A rich ruler, who enjoyed personal success as well as material blessings, approached Jesus to ask Him what he must do to inherit eternal life. Jesus responded by saying, "Thou knowest the commandments. Do not commit adultery, do not kill, do not steal, do not bear false witness, honour thy father and thy mother."

The man replied, "All these have I kept from my youth up." His apparent illusion of righteousness—that he had followed the law perfectly—certainly placed him in the high self-esteem category.

Jesus then told the man that he lacked the one thing necessary—to leave all and follow Him (Luke 18:18-25). But, the rich man was not willing to do that. Yes, he could follow an external Judeo-Christian type of ethic, but his own love and esteem of self prevented him from putting Christ first. He wanted all of what he already had and eternity too. That sounds like some who call themselves Christians today. They want it all now and eternity too.

The gospel of self-esteem would have had no appeal to Paul after his encounter with Christ. Nothing of self, even the very best that self could produce, could compare with knowing Christ. He declared:

> I count all things but loss for the excellency of the knowledge of Christ Jesus my Lord: for whom I have suffered the loss of all things, and do count them but dung, that I may win Christ, And be found in Him, not having mine own righteousness, which is of the law, but that which is through the faith of Christ, the righteousness which is of

God by faith: That I may know Him, and the power of His resurrection, and the fellowship of his sufferings, being made conformable unto His death. . . . I press toward the mark for the prize of the high calling of God in Christ Jesus (Philippians 3:8-10, 14).

To lose all to gain Christ does not lead to self-esteem, but to glory, where love for Jesus Christ eclipses self. Though Dobson claims to be biblical, his self-esteem teachings are not. Self-serving self-esteem teachings of Dobson and others only cause continued self-deception and self-bondage. Self-esteem, self-deception, and self-affirmation do not lead to truth or freedom in Christ. Those positive illusions may lead to self-hyphenated pseudoeuphoria and even worldly success, but they are not the truth that liberates. The painfully and precisely accurate truth about man should leave him hopeless apart from Christ.

But in Christ, a person discovers love—not self-love, but the love of God which passes understanding, which fills him with all the fullness of God. In Christ a person gains confidence—not self-confidence, but greater faith and confidence in Him and in the way He works through gifts He has given. In Christ a person finds contentment—not through self-acceptance, but through relationship with Jesus, who has promised never to leave him or forsake him. In Christ a person can live in righteousness and integrity—not through self-effort, self-righteousness or self-esteem, but because of the righteousness of Christ and because of His indwelling presence. In Christ a person experiences joy—not through circumstances or self-generated self-talk, but through relationship with Jesus and the fruit of the Spirit. Only in Christ does one find eternal life. All the rest is passing away like chaff blown by the wind.

Rather than creating a new race, God chose to redeem existing mankind. Rather than just fixing up persons, He made the grand exchange: His own life and character in place of fallen nature. Jesus made this ultimate conversion for His people on the basis of love. He emptied Himself and humbled Himself to become a man. He denied Himself by choosing to love. Through His death on the cross, He gave more love than we are able to receive. As we come to know Him, we recognize the shallowness and sinfulness of our own self-directed love in comparison with the vast consistency of His love and grace.

Rather than praying for believers to develop self-love and self-esteem, Paul prayed:

> That He would grant you, according to the riches of His glory, to be strengthened with might by His Spirit in the inner man; that Christ may dwell in your hearts by faith; that ye being rooted and grounded in love, may be able to comprehend with all saints what is the breadth, and length, and depth, and height; and to know the love of Christ, which passeth knowledge, that ye might be filled with all the fulness of God. Now unto Him that is able to do exceeding abundantly above all that we ask or think, according to the power that worketh in us, unto Him be glory in the church by Christ Jesus throughout all ages, world without end. Amen (Ephesians 3:16-21).

11

"Can You Trust Psychology?"

On his popular "Focus on the Family" radio program, Dobson discusses *Can You Trust Psychology?* with the author Dr. Gary Collins. Dobson praises Collins and his book and recommends it at the end of the broadcast. Collins' book is referred to as a quality resource.[1] Dobson and Collins discuss a number of topics from *Can You Trust Psychology?*

On Dobson's broadcast Collins complains that those of us who are critics of psychological counseling discourage individuals from seeing a psychotherapist. He says of those who have been influenced by the critics: "They are afraid to get the help they need."[2] We agree that we are opposed to their seeing a therapist, but for biblical reasons. We disagree with Collins and Dobson that those individuals would get the help they truly need through psychotherapy. Dobson's response to Collins' concern about individuals failing to get help "that they really need" is: "That can be dangerous." We disagree and believe that the research does not support such a conclusion.[3]

Dobson follows with five examples which illustrate how much he grossly misunderstands the position of the critics of psychology. It may be that he is too busy to read the critics. If so, he should not pretend to understand when he does not. He says, "Here are examples of individuals who will be in very deep weeds if there is no help for them within the field of counseling or psychology."[4]

Before we look at his examples we wish to reiterate our position. We say:

> When we speak of psychology we are **not** referring to the entire discipline of psychology. Instead we are speaking about that part of psychology which deals with the very nature of man, how he should live, and how he should change. This includes psychological counseling, clinical counseling, psychotherapy, and the psychological aspects of psychiatry. . . .
>
> We believe that mental-emotional-behavioral problems of living (nonorganic problems) should be ministered to by biblical encouragement, exhortation, preaching, teaching, and counseling which depends solely upon the truth of God's Word without incorporating the unproven and unscientific psychological opinions of men. Then, if there are biological, medical problems, the person should seek medical rather than psychological assistance.[5]

We further say:

> The opposing position varies from the sole use of psychology without the use of any Scripture to an integration of the two in varying amounts, depending upon the personal judgment of the individual. Integration is the attempt to combine theories, ideas, and opinions from psychotherapy, clinical psychology, counseling psychology, and their underlying psychologies with Scripture. Christian integrationists use psychological opinions about the nature of man, why he does what he does, and how he can change, in ways that seem to them to be compatible with their Christian faith or their view of the Bible. They may quote from the Bible, utilize certain

biblical principles, and attempt to stay within what they consider to be Christian or biblical guidelines. Nevertheless, they do not have confidence in the Word of God for all matters of life, conduct, and counseling. Therefore they use the secular psychological theories and techniques in what they would consider to be a Christian way.[6]

A "Psychotic Break"?

Now for Dobson's examples. He gives his first example as follows:

> The woman who experiences a psychotic break with reality and runs screaming down the middle of the road, when apprehended. She babbles incoherently and then curls up in a fetal position for days at a time. Should a husband take her to their pastor for counseling? That's one of the recommendations that are often in those books, that pastors should be able to handle it.[7]

Let's consider the possibility, along with Dobson, that the woman only needs counseling or talk therapy. If so, we have already shown elsewhere that research indicates that a pastor is as likely to be a help or hindrance as a psychological counselor.[8]

This is another of Dobson's weaknesses in that he believes the secular mythology about counseling and then promotes it among Christians. He does not name individuals whom he regards as critics and he seems loath to quote any research to support what he says.

Let us look at research studies that demonstrate how professionals (licensed, trained therapists) compare with amateurs, such as pastors. In comparing amateurs and professionals with respect to therapeutic effectiveness, Dr. Joseph Durlak found in 40 out of 42 studies that the results produced by the amateurs were equal to or better than by the profession-als![9] In a four-volume series called *The Regulation of Psychotherapists*,[10] Dr. Daniel Hogan, a social psychologist at Harvard, analyzed the traits and qualities that characterize psychotherapists. In half of the studies amateurs did better than professionals.[11] Research psychiatrist Dr. Jerome Frank reveals the shocking fact that research has not proven that pro-fessionals produce better results than amateurs.[12]

Dr. Hans Eysenck declares:

> It is unfortunate for the well-being of psychology as a science that . . . the great majority of psychologists, who after all are practicing clinicians, will pay no attention whatsoever to the negative outcome of all the studies carried on over the past thirty years but will continue to use methods which have by now not only failed to find evidence in support of their effectiveness, but for which there is now ample evidence that they are no better than placebo treatments.

Eysenck continues:

> Do we really have the right to impose a lengthy training on medical doctors and psychologists in order to enable them to practice a skill which has no practical relevance to the curing of neurotic disorders? Do we have the right to charge patients fees, or get the State to pay us for a treatment which is no better than a placebo?[13]

It is too bad that Dobson is ignorant of such research or, if aware, gives no indication of it in his speaking and writing.

Learning Problem

For his second example, Dobson says:

The eight-year-old boy who can't learn to read and is being shredded by his peers at school. Does he have a visual-perceptual problem? Is he retarded? Is he dyslexic? Can we help him learn? Is his pastor equipped to answer those questions? Usually not. Now here again, see, psychology is so broad I think the people who write those books think only of a psychotherapeutic approach.[14]

As the reader can see from the previous explanation of our position, this problem is unrelated to our target of criticism. If the case is a biological problem, the boy should see a medical doctor. If it is an educational problem, he should see someone who could give him the best help for the least amount of money.

If this is a motivational problem, which could involve a variety of factors, we would suggest an interested person who could encourage and help the boy. We can see the possible use of a medical doctor, or educator, a family member or friend. We would not recommend a psychotherapist as it would be unnecessary and possibly destructive.

Dobson's bringing in the boy with the educational problem and then mentioning the possibility of it being a visual-perceptual problem, a retardation problem, a dyslexic problem, a learning problem and suggesting that this kind of psychology is involved is further evidence of his ignorance of what the criticism is really about. This may be a convenient ignorance that permits him to avoid dealing with the real problem and the real criticism. The real problem is how to deal with problems of living and the real question is this: Is the Bible sufficient to deal with problems of living as Christians thought right up to the rise of psychology in the current century? Obviously Dobson thinks not.

Sexual Impotence

Dobson's third example of a problem is:

The man who is sexually impotent, frustrating his wife and condemning himself in embarrassment and anger. Again, will his pastor be able to uncover and resolve his problem? Probably not.[15]

The Harvard Medical School Mental Health Letter states

Sexual problems are caused less often by sheer ignorance than by lack of confidence, obsessive self-observation, anxiety about performance, conditioned responses, or cultural inhibitions.[16]

Here again Dobson is throwing out a condition that could be as simple as a medical problem and as complex as a host of biological, mental and environmental problems. If it is solely a medical problem, is Dobson suggesting the man see a psychological counselor? Maybe so, but hopefully not. If it is not solely biological, then Dobson is put to the test. Would he send the man to a psychological counselor? We think so. We would recommend against it. We have enough confidence in individuals who use Scripture to deal with such problems and enough research to support the idea that professionals would likely not do better than a lay person. Many pastors **could** help. Dobson, like most "Christian psychologists," tends to demean pastors.

Celibate Homosexual

The fourth example is:

The celibate homosexual who wants more than anything in his life to change—and there are those individuals out there—but he has no idea how to start. He has prayed for years, but illicit desire is still within him. Where does he turn? To whom does he discuss those things?[17]

In this series of examples, Dobson mentions sending someone to the Minirth-Meier Clinic in Dallas. Let's use them as an
example of psychological treatment for homosexuality. In our
book *Prophets of PsychoHeresy I*, we show that Paul Meier and
Frank Minirth are Freudian in their view of homosexuality.
Dobson exhibits great confidence in these two men. Our confidence is in God's Word and the work of the Holy Spirit to deal
with such problems, not in Freud and his unproven notions. We
are sorry that Dobson, Meier and Minirth lack this confidence
in Scripture and in God's promises.

Depression

The fifth and last example from this broadcast is:

> The seventy-year-old man with whom I worked this past
> year. He had recently retired from the ministry and he
> was mired in unrelenting depression. He cried through-
> out every day. Some might have criticized his weakness
> and self pity. Instead, I referred him to the excellent
> Christian psychiatric clinic of Minirth-Meier in Dallas
> Texas. These doctors who spend four hours every day
> studying Scripture.[18]

The problem apparently was that the man "suffered a
series of small strokes deep within his brain." Dobson says:
"Thank God for these Christian psychiatrists who identified the
problem. His pastor could not and did not help."[19] Now really!
Dobson has gone off the deep end on this type of reasoning. The
problem apparently had a biological source. It is not only true
that "his pastor could not help," but also true that a psychological counselor could not help either. A pastor is as able and as
likely to suggest a medical check-up as a psychological counselor may be. Dobson is using a medical problem to establish a
need for psychological counseling. Incredible!

Incidentally, if Paul Meier "spends four hours a day study-ing Scripture," as Dobson alleges, it is sad that he and Minirth support Freudian psychology to the extent they do. One would think that studying Scripture four hours a day would lead to more confidence in Scripture rather than confidence in the opinions of men such as Freud. In addition, we have shown elsewhere that Meier and Minirth's exegetical conclusions result in unbiblical ideas.[20]

On the same broadcast, Mike Trout says:

> People will go to a tennis professional to take tennis lessons, they go take golf lessons if they want to learn how to improve their golf game, but they won't go to a professional in the area of life's problems to help them in their own personal day to day living.[21]

This is just another confusion of the physical and tangible (tennis and golf) and the spiritual (problems of living). With this type of confused reasoning one could end up taking his automobile to a psychologist for repair. Mind and brain are not the same; issues and tissues are not the same; and problems of living and tennis or golf are not the same. Failure to distin-guish tennis and problems of living are ignorance enough. But, to advertise this ignorance to numerous others is doubly unfor-tunate. And—who is **God's** professional when it comes to prob-lems of living? God has called mature Christians, not psychologists, to this task.

These five examples demonstrate Dobson's weak and fuzzy thinking and further demonstrate that he is ignorant of the criticism of the use of psychological counseling. His contrived examples stand as straw men that fall apart in the midst of his erecting them. He confuses the biological, mental and environ-mental, shows little respect for the ministry, and reveals his overwhelming confidence in psychological theories and thera-pies over God's Word and ways.

Professional Psychological Counselors

During the second day of the broadcast, Dobson and Collins discuss seeking a professional and Christians becoming psychological counselors. Dobson asks, "When specifically should you look for a person with professional credentials?"[22] In response, Collins says:

> Suppose you're not getting better, suppose the problem is not changing. Maybe if the problem seems to be rather severe, psychologically severe, you're showing unusual behavior. Many times the problem is physical and if you sense there is anything physical, but I think in general, if you're just not getting better from talking to a lay person, then it is time to seek out some professional guidance.[23]

Yes, there are problems that do not change when seeing a lay person. No doubt about it. The same happens in "professional" counseling. There is no question that there are problems that do not change when seeing a professional counselor either. Why is it that this possibility is not mentioned by Dobson and Collins? Probably because they both have a psychological mind-set.

And would they even think to state the reverse of their example? Would they recommend someone who is seeing a professional to switch to a lay person if there is no improvement? We don't think so. In fact, the idea probably never crossed their minds. The usual recommendation given by psychologists for a person who is not being helped by a professional is to find another professional.

Contrary to what Dobson and Collins believe, the idea that the "psychologically severe" problems should be sent to a professional is **not** supported by the research. **In fact the research indicates that psychotherapy works best for those who need it least.**[24]

Dobson and Collins stress training in order to become a professional counselor. However, the research regarding the relationship between training and effectiveness is such that it is surprising that either Dobson or Collins would recommend additional training as a means of helping people. As we explained earlier in this chapter, the research reveals that amateurs (such as friends, relatives, neighbors) do at least as well as professionals.

"Christian Psychology"

Dobson says, "There are some writers who are going around the country telling them that there is no such thing as Christian Psychology."[25] Unfortunately what has been labeled "Christian psychology" is made up of the very same confusion of contradictory theories and techniques as secular psychology. Well-meaning psychologists who profess Christianity have merely borrowed the theories and techniques from secular psychology. They dispense what they believe to be the perfect blend of psychology and Christianity. Nevertheless, the psychology they use is the same as that used by non-Christian psychologists and psychiatrists. They use the theories and techniques devised by such men as Freud, Jung, Rogers, Janov, Ellis, Adler, Berne, Fromm, Maslow, and others, none of whom embraced Christianity or developed a psychological system from the Word of God.

The Christian Association for Psychological Studies (CAPS) is a group of psychologists and psychological counselors who are professing Christians. At one of their meetings the following was said:

> We are often asked if we are "Christian psychologists" and find it difficult to answer since we don't know what the question implies. We are Christians who are psychologists but at the present time there is no acceptable Christian psychology that is markedly different from non-Christian psychology. It is difficult to imply that we function in a manner that is fundamentally distinct from our

non-Christian colleagues. . . . as yet there is not an acceptable theory, mode of research or treatment methodology that is distinctly Christian.[26]

Although Christian psychological counselors claim to have taken only those elements of psychology that fit with Christianity, by bending the Bible anything can be made to fit, no matter how silly or even satanic it is. Each Christian therapist brings his own individual psychology (borrowed from the world) to the Bible and modifies the Word to make it fit. What they use comes from the bankrupt systems of ungodly and unscientific theories and techniques.

Christians who seek to integrate psychology with Christianity have actually turned to secular, ungodly sources for help. But, because these unbiblical, unsubstantiated theories and techniques have been blended into the dough, they are well hidden in the loaf. Thus many Christians honestly believe they are using only a purified, Christianized psychology. Instead, they are left with a contaminated loaf, not with the unleavened bread of the Word of God.

In contrast, A. W. Tozer declares:

At the heart of the Christian system lies the cross of Christ with its divine paradox. The power of Christianity appears in its antipathy toward, never in its agreement with, the ways of fallen men. . . . The cross stands in bold opposition to the natural man. Its philosophy runs contrary to the processes of the unregenerate mind, so that Paul could say bluntly that the preaching of the cross is to them that perish foolishness. To try to find a common ground between the message of the cross and man's fallen reason is to try the impossible, and if persisted in must result in an impaired reason, a meaningless cross and a powerless Christianity.[27]

Can You Trust Psychology?

Dobson continues his interview with Collins by saying, "Jesus and Paul never used psychology. Why should we?"[28] Collins replies:

> Jesus never used radio. . . . God in His wisdom gives us tools that we can use. And radio is maybe the most obvious example for us today. But there are many things, many tools that we've got, many gifts that we've got.[29]

Collins discusses this issue in his book which Dobson recommends. In that book, Collins engages in a number of confusions that are typical among Christians who are enamored of psychological counseling and its underlying psychologies. He says, "In mathematics, medicine, physics, geography, marine biology and a host of other areas there is much truth that is not mentioned in the Bible."[30] Collins uses this statement to add to his continual analogy of science and psychology.

It is understandable that real science is useful in revealing the physical universe to us. The Bible is neither a physics book nor a chemistry book, but it is most emphatically a book about God and man. It is the only book that contains uncontaminated truth about man, his problems in living and God's solutions to them—whereas psychological counseling theories are only opinions.

Dr. Karl Popper, considered by many to be the greatest twentieth-century philosopher of science, has examined psychological theories having to do with understanding and treating human behavior. He says that these theories, "though posing as sciences, had in fact more in common with primitive myths than with science; that they resembled astrology rather than astronomy." He says, "These theories describe some facts but in the manner of myths. They contain most interesting psychological suggestions, but not in testable form."[31]

Popper is not alone in this conclusion. Psychologist Carol Tavris says:

Now the irony is that many people who are not fooled by astrology for one minute subject themselves to therapy for years, where the same errors of logic and interpretation often occur.[32]

Research psychiatrist Jerome Frank also equates psychotherapies with myths because "they are not subject to disproof."[33] One can develop a theory for explaining all human behavior and then interpret all behavior in the light of that explanation. This not only applies to psychology but to graphology, astrology, and other such "ologies" as well.

For an area of study to qualify as a science, there must be the possibility of not only refuting theories but also predicting future events, reproducing results obtained, and controlling what is observed. Lewis Thomas says, "Science requires, among other things, a statistically significant number of reproducible observations and, above all, controls."[34]

When one moves from the natural sciences to the "behavioral sciences," there is also a move away from refutability, predictability, reproducibility, and controllability. Furthermore, the cause and effect relationship, so evident in the natural sciences, is ambiguous or absent in the "behavioral sciences." Instead of causation (cause and effect), psychotherapy rests heavily upon covariation (events which appear together which may not necessarily be related).

To support his position that this type of psychology is science, Collins fails to mention one philosopher of science, one Nobel Laureate, or one distinguished professor who supports his subjectively held personal view, which is propagated by fiat rather than fact. Yet he continues to refer to such theories as "scientific conclusions."[35]

Because those psychological theories are not "scientific conclusions" and because propagators of such theories and therapies claim to have special knowledge about the human condition and how to deal with problems of living, Dr. Garth Wood is concerned about those who come under their influence. He says in his book *The Myth of Neurosis:*

Cowed by their status as men of science, deferring to their academic titles, bewitched by the initials after their names, we, the gullible, lap up their pretentious nonsense as if it were the gospel truth. We must learn to recognize them for what they are—possessors of no special knowledge of the human psyche, who have nonetheless, chosen to earn their living from the dissemination of the myth that they do indeed know how the mind works, are thoroughly conversant with the "rules" that govern human behavior. . . . To take money for mere talk is, I would argue, in many cases both negligent and, despite the purest of motives, irresponsible.[36]

Collins continues his error in logic when he equates using psychology with using modern technology, such as the radio and antibiotics. He argues that Jesus and Paul didn't use modern technology, not because it was wrong, but because it was not available, with the implication that the only reason Jesus and Paul did not avail themselves of psychology is because it was not available then.[37]

Elsewhere, however, Collins admits that Jesus and Paul would not have used psychology even if it had been available. Of Jesus he says:

If psychology had been taught at the universities when he walked on the earth, Jesus probably would not have taken a course because he didn't have to. His knowledge of human behavior was infinite and perfect.[38]

Note that Collins says, "probably would not." Apparently he isn't sure. Furthermore, Jesus' knowledge is still infinite and perfect. That is why a mature Christian will rely on Jesus dwelling in him and guiding the ministry of God's Word—something that seems foreign to both Dobson and Collins.

Concerning Paul, Collins admits:

Paul, in contrast, did not have Jesus' infinite understanding, but he was a well-educated intellectual who understood many of the world's philosophies. He rejected the notion that these could give ultimate answers to human questions. Instead he built many of his arguments on Scripture and insisted that the scholars of his time repent. Surely the apostle would have presented a similar message to psychological scholars if they had existed when Paul was alive.[39]

Indeed, Paul would have opposed the inclusion of psychological explanations of man. Psychology evolved out of philosophy and Paul warns against using the vain philosophies of men (Colossians 2:8). Nevertheless, in spite of his admission, Collins asks:

Does it follow, however, that the modern disciple of Christ and reader of Paul's epistles should throw away psychology books and reject psychology because it was not used centuries ago?[40]

Regarding the type of psychology we criticize, we would have to answer a strong **yes**, because they did not use it centuries ago for the same reasons they would not use it now. Are we to change the intent of Scripture simply because we are living in a different century?

On Dobson's broadcast Collins continues his discussion by referring to the woman in the Bible with the issue of blood, whom physicians could not help. He says:

It may very well have been solved very easily today, because God has allowed us, and I say us, meaning the human race, and sometimes He has taught us some marvelous things about the human body through modern medicine and research done by non-Christians.[41]

Collins is simply restating his confused thinking from his book, in which he says of the Christian counselor,

> When such a person does counseling, he or she may use techniques that some consider secular—just as the Christian physician uses "secular" medical techniques, the Christian banker uses "secular" banking methods, and the Christian legislator uses "secular" approaches to lawmaking.[42]

Collins constantly creates a parallel between the psychological and the medical. However, one is in the realm of science (medical) and the other is not. Equating the practice of medicine with the practice of psychology shows little sensitivity to the gross errors involved in this mistaken logic. The error is compounded throughout Collins' book.[43]

Medical Model Confusion

By comparing the practice of psychological counseling with medicine, psychologists often use the medical model to justify the use of psychotherapy. By using the medical model, many assume that "mental illness" can be thought of and talked about in the same manner and terms as medical illness. After all, both are called "illnesses." However, in the medical model physical symptoms are caused by some pathogenic agent, such as viruses. Remove the pathogenic agent and the symptoms go as well. Or, a person may have a broken leg; set the leg according to learned techniques and the leg will heal. One tends to have confidence in this model because it has worked well in treating physical ailments. With the easy transfer of the model from the medical world to the psychotherapeutic world, many people believe that mental problems are the same as physical problems.

Applying the medical model to psychotherapy originated with the relationship between psychiatry and medicine. Since psychiatrists are medical doctors and since psychiatry is a medical specialty, it seemed to follow that the medical model applied to psychiatry just as it did to medicine. Furthermore, psychiatry is draped with such medical trimmings as offices in medical clinics, hospitalization of patients, diagnostic services, prescription drugs, and therapeutic treatment. The very word *therapy* implies medical treatment. Further expansion of the use of the medical model to all psychological counseling was easy after that.

The practice of medicine deals with the physical, biological aspects of a person; psychotherapy deals with the spiritual, social, mental, and emotional aspects. Whereas medical doctors attempt to heal the body, psychotherapists attempt to alleviate or cure emotional, mental, and even spiritual suffering and to establish new patterns of personal and social behavior. In spite of such differences, Dobson, Collins and others continue to call upon the medical model to support the activities of the psychotherapist.

Additionally, the medical model supports the idea that every person with social or mental problems is ill. When people are labeled "mentally ill," problems of living are categorized under the key term *mental illness*. Dr. Thomas Szasz explains it this way: "If we now classify certain forms of personal conduct as illness, it is because most people believe that the best way to deal with them is by responding to them as if they were medical diseases."[44]

Those who believe this do so because they have been influenced by the medical model of human behavior and are confused by the terminology. They think that if one can have a sick body, it must follow that one can have a sick mind. But, is the mind part of the body? Or can we equate the mind with the body? The authors of the *Madness Establishment* say, "Unlike many medical diseases that have scientifically verifiable etiologies and prescribed methods of treatment, most of the 'mental illnesses' have neither scientifically established causes nor treatments of proven efficacy."[45]

In concluding Part Three of his book *Can You Trust Psychology?* Collins says, "It is too early to answer decisively if psychology and Christianity can be integrated."[46] If one agrees with Collins, one is compelled to ask the question, "Then why integrate?" However, we disagree with Collins. It is **not** too early. Based on hundreds of research studies, Dr. Robyn Dawes, professor at Carnegie-Mellon University and a widely recognized researcher on psychological evaluations, declares:

> . . . there is no positive evidence supporting the efficacy of professional psychology. There are anecdotes, there is plausibility, there are common beliefs, yes—but there is no good evidence.[47]

With the literally thousands of research studies on psychotherapy and its underlying psychologies and the lack of support as a result, it seems obvious that it should **not** be integrated with Christianity. Neither Dobson nor Collins has presented credible evidence to support this integration of psychology and Christianity.

12

Dr. Dobson Answers His Critics

A question and answer section of a book about Dobson once more demonstrates how stuck he is on the humanistic notions of self-esteem, self-etc. He sees situations through his own erroneous unsubstantiated conclusion that low-self-esteem leads to social problems. That question and answer section contains some of the same information as from his tape "Raising Confident Kids in an Age of Inferiority"[1] and a recent two-day broadcast entitled "A Biblical View of Self-Esteem."[2]

A question from that book and his response are quite revealing. The question raised is this:

> Speaking of *Hide or Seek*, that book is about building self-esteem in children. You have been criticized in recent years for being the guru of self-esteem, which some of your critics consider to be unbiblical.[3]

We will examine several facets of Dobson's response. He says, "Yes, I am aware of this criticism, and some of it appears deliberately designed to distort my beliefs and teachings."[4] Unfortunately no one is quoted. Therefore the reader is not able to see if Dobson's statement is true. This is an example of how difficult it is to confront him when he does not name individuals or footnote what he says. It is a common weakness in his writings.

We are familiar with the few who criticize Dobson but we know of no one who has "deliberately designed to distort" his "beliefs and teachings." Simple courtesy on his part, let alone academic necessity, would require that he quote the critics and demonstrate that there is deliberate distortion of his beliefs and teachings. We hope he will eventually begin to do this.

As to the number of his critics, Dobson himself admits to hardly ever being criticized. In a letter to two authors who mentioned him briefly in a book he says, "400,000 copies of the book [*Hide or Seek*] have sold in Christian circles, yet you're only the third person ever to raise the issues you now feel are overwhelmingly unbiblical."[5]

Rolf Zettersten, as Senior Vice President of Focus on the Family, says:

> Dr. James Dobson and the ministry of Focus on the Family have never been the subject of heated controversy within the Christian community—at least, not to the time of this writing. He receives only two negative letters out of every one thousand arriving at his Pomona headquarters, and some of those are directed at his radio guests.[6]

The former ("only the third person") seems to refer to public criticism; while the latter is obviously private criticism (by letter). As we have argued in this volume, his unbiblical and unscientific stand on self-esteem and psychology deserves more criticism than it draws.

> If I am *anything*, I am an orthodox, mainline evangelical in my thought and writings. I would never do or say anything I felt was contradictory to Scripture.[7] (Emphasis his.)

Criticisms of Dobson do not deny that he presents himself as "orthodox, mainline evangelical in" his "thoughts and writings." Our criticism is not directed at what Dobson hopes to accomplish or what he thinks about himself; it is directed at what he actually teaches. As we have shown, he does say things contrary to Scripture, as well as to current research.

After describing in a negative way an era of "me-ism," Dobson says:

> . . . several Christian authors and speakers now make a decent living by going around the country telling people that I believe and promote this kind of humanistic psychobabble.[8]

While we do know a few Christian authors and speakers who criticize Dobson, we know none that "make a decent living" at it. In fact, those we know who critique Dobson realize they could make a decent living just by "going around the country" praising his teachings. We hardly need to say who is more popular, Dr. James Dobson or his critics. Count the number of copies of his books sold, magazines circulated, material distributed, and hundreds of staff members at Focus on the Family. Compare it with his critics. One wonders why he makes so much ado about his few critics, unless it serves as a means to rally additional support.

As to his critics believing that he is promoting humanistic psychobabble, he is correct. As we have indicated earlier, Dobson does buy and market humanistic psychobabble. The sad thing about it is that he continues to invent straw men on the subject of self-esteem and then proceeds to knock them down. However, to our knowledge Dobson never has had a public interchange with any of his critics regarding his version of humanistic psychobabble. It would seem to us that his supporters would encourage such an interchange so that his critics would be silenced once and for all. . . unless, of course, Dobson is shown to be wrong.

Dobson says:

My book *Hide or Seek*, which has been singled out as an example of this heresy, relates not to me-ism at all, but to the protection of a child's emotional apparatus during the particularly vulnerable years of his development. Rather than recommending the elevation of ourselves, I was trying in that book to help parents protect their children from the epidemic of self-hatred that has besieged an entire generation of young people.[9]

However, research on positive illusions and self-deception, discussed earlier, certainly does **not** support Dobson's statement about "the existence of self-hatred that has besieged an entire generation of young people."

Such research reported by Dr. Shelley Taylor in her book *Positive Illusions* indicates that children naturally begin to enhance their self-esteem early in life through positive illusion. Furthermore, the Bible says, "Foolishness is bound in the heart of a child; but the rod of correction shall drive it far from him" (Proverbs 22:15). Coupled with Jeremiah 17:9 and other verses, we see the actual condition of the child. If Dobson has biblical or scientific support for his position he should provide it, rather than repeating seemingly reckless rhetoric about what he thinks to be true.

Dobson justifies *Hide or Seek* with an extreme example of a girl called Tracy.[10] He is a past master at contriving passionate dramas of extreme examples to prove his points. He gives this one example as evidence of the "epidemic of self-hatred." However, even if this contrived example were true, it represents a case of low self-esteem that is in the minority. In addition, Tracy may not even have what is called low self-esteem; instead, she may be what Dobson refers to as "brokenhearted." In other words, she might be hurt and discouraged, but not be in a state of low self-esteem.

We generally agree with Dobson when he says, "If there is one thing this brokenhearted kid needs, it is a friend . . . someone who would say, 'I understand; I care; I love you and God loves you.'"[11] But we disagree with Dobson when he says, "She

[Tracy] also needs a book like *Hide or Seek* that will tell her parents about her pain and will offer some suggestions for reducing it."[12] We disagree with him because his book presents humanistic psychobabble that is not needed and may be detrimental. What Tracy and her parents need is the Lord Himself, new life in Him and the fruit of the Spirit of that new life. They need someone who will come alongside and disciple them in the Word of God, unadulterated by the amalgamation of psychological notions and nonsense.

Dobson continues:

> What she doesn't need is a noncaring biblical analysis from a person who has never counseled such a kid in his life, saying that God prefers humiliation to adequacy. I don't believe it.[13]

We agree that she "doesn't need" a "noncaring biblical analysis." But how about biblical love and how about showing Tracy God's love in action? He mentions "a person who has never counseled such a kid," but to whom is he referring? How about a person who has ministered to numerous such kids, but who has a different view of Tracy than Dobson's and a different solution? A biblical solution, not a biblicized humanistic solution.

When Dobson refers to people "saying God prefers humiliation to adequacy," he evidently confuses humiliation with humility. The Bible very clearly puts humility above confidence in the flesh (self-confidence, self-esteem, etc.). Psalm 34:18 says, "The LORD is nigh unto them that are of a broken heart; and saveth such as be of a contrite spirit." This is repeated in Psalm 51:17. Isaiah 57:15 says:

> For thus saith the high and lofty One that inhabiteth eternity, whose name is Holy; I dwell in the high and holy place, with him also that is of a contrite and humble spirit, to revive the spirit of the humble, and to revive the heart of the contrite ones.

Our adequacy is to be in the Lord, not in ourselves.

> Thus saith the LORD; Cursed be the man that trusteth in man, and maketh flesh his arm, and whose heart departeth from the LORD. . . .Blessed is the man that trusteth in the LORD, and whose hope the LORD is (Jeremiah 17:5, 7).

If a parent brings up his child in the nurture and admonition of the Lord, he will love and esteem the child, but not attempt to build his illusions of self-esteem. He will desire to guide the child into finding his adequacy in the Lord and not in himself. This is not an easy thing to do. It is much easier to build a child's self-esteem than to disciple him into walking in the Spirit rather than according to the flesh. As we have shown, self-deception to sustain self-esteem is the norm rather than the exception.

Directly following the extreme example of Tracy, Dobson says:

> Tens of thousands of these teenagers are killing themselves every year because they can see no reason to go on living. Others sink into drug abuse, sexual immorality, and crime. The common denominator among them is a personal revulsion that goes to the very core of their being. And for the life of me, I can't see how it can be considered "unbiblical" to try to protect them from a social system that perpetuates this hatred![14]

From a single, extreme, unsupportable-as-epidemic example, Dobson concludes that all of these teenagers are killing themselves because "they can see no reason to go on living." The common denominator to teen suicide, drug abuse, sexual immorality and crime is a "personal revulsion," or as he would amplify, low-self-esteem and feelings of inferiority. If this were true, there should be proof for it in the research.

Dobson's followers believe it must be true because "Dr. Dobson says so." However, Dobson needs more than his say-so to make it true for those who require biblical support or scientific evidence. Dobson depends on his rhetoric without research to be received uncritically by his followers, and unfortunately it is. In spite of the few critics (made to sound like many), Dobson is listened to, accepted, endorsed, and financially supported by myriads of people across the country.

Let us examine the areas of teenage suicide, drug abuse, sexual immorality and crime mentioned by Dobson. We already mentioned **the lack of support for connecting those social ills to low self-esteem** when we quoted Dr. Neil Smelser's summary from the research volume by the California Task Force on Self-Esteem. We now look at some additional findings from that volume as well as from other research.

Teenage Suicide

If Dobson has research to support the relationship between low self-esteem, feelings of inferiority (or whatever other name he wishes to use) and suicide, he should provide it. Suicides do occur among those who are **labeled** as having low self-esteem, but so do they occur among those who are regarded as having high levels of self-esteem. Both are found in the research literature. However, it would be erroneous and irresponsible to connect either low or high self-esteem to suicide without extensive and exhaustive research support.

The Social Importance of Self-Esteem reports:

> Suicidal behavior and the need for self-destructive relationships suggest serious problems with self-concept. But so do narcissistic disorders in which people appear to have very high levels of self-esteem, while behaving with arrogance and disregard for others.[15]

While no one has directly shown that low self-esteem causes suicide, there are studies that show that alcohol is involved in nearly half of the suicides.[16] We also know from the research that some therapists have precipitated suicide. Dr. Jonas Robitscher, in his book *The Powers of Psychiatry*, says:

> A therapist may make angry or ill-timed or incorrect interpretations, stir up hostility that his patient is unable to tolerate, and then angrily reject the patient, who may then fall into a suicidal depression. When patients are suicidal, sometimes the indifferent, flippant, or hostile attitude of the therapist or of the hospital staff precipitates a suicide attempt. Joseph Andriola has suggested that when seriously suicidal patients are not taken seriously or are disparaged by doctors and hospital staff, "such attitudes and the messages they convey strip the patients of any remaining shred of hope and provide him with a license for the attempted self-murder."[17]

However, that does not mean that one can generalize and say that tens of thousands of patients are committing suicide in response to therapy.

We also know that psychiatrists seem to be at the top of the list of men in various occupations who suicide.[18] However, while we know the incidence of suicide, we do not know the reason or reasons. Thus, we cannot conclude that their suicides are a result of low self-esteem or high self-esteem, or feelings of inferiority or feelings of superiority.

It is sad that so many people who listen to Dobson receive what he says but do not insist upon evidence of any kind. There is an old criticism about an individual who "jumps to conclusions," but we wonder if Dobson jumps to confusions. Without support and in all seriousness, he connects low self-esteem and suicide. This is a conclusion that is a confusion of cause and effect.

Drug Abuse

One researcher says:

> . . . there is a paucity of good research, especially studies
> that could link the abuse of alcohol and drugs with self-
> esteem. What evidence there is remains inconsistent.[19]

He continues:

> Empirical studies concerning the relationship between
> alcohol and drug abuse and self-esteem show mixed
> results.[20]

A report on Diana Baumrind's study which compared both
discipline and self-esteem with drug use reveals:

> Children of "democratic" parents, who were supported
> but not highly controlled, also **scored high on all self-
> esteem and competence measures but were likelier
> to become heavily involved with drugs**.[21] (Emphasis
> added.)

Sexual Immorality

Two researchers say:

> Although there is no evidence that self-esteem directly
> affects sexual behavior, there is evidence that age of first
> intercourse tends to be earlier for adolescents with **lower
> school achievement**. Thus, raising achievement level
> might be expected to influence sexual behavior. More-
> over, individuals with high self-esteem may decide to
> become sexually active for reasons different from those of
> individuals with low self-esteem. For example, an adoles-
> cent with high self-esteem may engage in sex because she

is involved in a loving relationship, whereas an adolescent with low self-esteem may do so because she is afraid of being rejected.[22] (Emphasis added.)

These researchers say, "Available research linking low self-esteem with adolescent pregnancy is suggestive, rather than compelling."[23] They also admit a need for longitudinal studies. Without well-constructed longitudinal studies for support, it would be foolish to connect low self-esteem with sexual behavior, or drug abuse, or suicide or anything else.

Crime

Three researchers say:

> . . . most research conducted outside the laboratory has attempted only to demonstrate correlations between levels of self-esteem and behavior, showing the possibility of a relationship without establishing causation. Even with such a limited goal, the correlations reported have been weak at best. Clearly, longitudinal studies are required to ascertain whether level of self-esteem plays a *causal* role in violent or criminal behavior. Very few such studies have been conducted.[24] (Emphasis theirs.)

The researchers say that family violence crimes **may** (meaning that they do not know for sure) be related to self-esteem. However, they also say:

> . . . in crimes against property and against the public order, the connection with self-esteem is not clear. This is not to say there is no connection; rather, studies simply do not provide a clear picture.[25]

One research study supported by the National Institute of Mental Health attempted to find a relationship between self-esteem and delinquent children. The researchers concluded that "the effect of self-esteem on delinquent behavior is negligible." The researchers say, "Given the extensive speculation and debate about self-esteem and delinquency, we find these results something of an embarrassment."[26]

Self-Hatred

Dobson's final statement in the paragraph quoted earlier is:

> And for the life of me, I can't see how it can be considered "unbiblical" to try to protect them [teenagers] from a social system that perpetuates this hatred![27]

Dobson's final statement in the paragraph is dependent upon a connection between low self-esteem and social problems which has not been proven. In addition it seems that the Adamic human tendency toward self-aggrandizement is what we need to be worried about and not self-hatred.

Dobson concludes:

> If there is no such thing as low self-esteem—no condition known as self-hatred—no overwhelming feelings of inadequacy and inferiority—then it stands to reason that a child cannot be damaged by the stressful experiences of childhood. If there are no wounded spirits and damaged egos, it is impossible to hurt a child emotionally.[28]

This sentence contains the words *self-esteem, self-hatred, feelings of inferiority*. Those are the concepts through which Dobson sees individuals and, in this case, children. To begin with, it does not, to use his words, "stand to reason" that without low self-esteem, self-hatred, and feelings of inferiority "that a child cannot be damaged by the stressful experiences of childhood." Further, if one eliminated both low and high self-esteem, both self-love and self-hatred, and feelings of both inferiority and superiority there would still be children "damaged by the stressful experiences of childhood."

There are numerous reasons why children suffer, including social isolation, inadequate parenting, a sense of helplessness, poor body image, an inability to trust others, an inability to express feelings, a lack of control over one's environment, and so on. Dobson's assumption that low self-esteem, self-hatred and feelings of inferiority are the only possible factors relating to children being "damaged by the stressful experiences of childhood" is a massively mistaken one. Therefore his conclusions are spurious.

Dobson then goes on to a superlative, nonsensical diatribe against the person who would dare challenge his connection of low self-esteem and damaged children. We can only say that he has come to a factitious conclusion through fictitious reasoning. He says:

> He is impervious to alcoholic parents or abusing adults who tell him he is ugly, unwanted, unloved, and destined to fail in everything he does. When the pedophile strips a boy or girl naked and photographs them with pistols or mousetraps on the body, it does not damage their self-esteem! When unwanted kids are bounced from one rejecting home to another, it does not affect their self-concept! When an adolescent is laughed at every day of his life and is never invited or included or respected, it only serves to inflate his ego! The only problem is that such a person is puffed up with concealed pride! That is pure nonsense, and I'm pleased that very few people seem to believe it.[29]

It is sad to see how few people can see through Dobson's prestidigitations and perambulations of prose in order to promote his perverted pronouncements.

That children can be and are harmed by cruelty and rejection does not prove the need for self-esteem. It shows the need for esteeming others more than self. It demonstrates the depravity of man and the need of a Savior. The answer to the grief that so many suffer is found in the Gospel of Jesus Christ for the redemption of sinful, suffering souls and ongoing process of sanctification, in which Christians walk according to the Spirit rather than the flesh, confess and forgive sins, and love God and others by the enabling of the Holy Spirit dwelling in them.

13

The Primrose Path

Where will psychology and selfology with its self-esteem, self-affirmation, and self-serving bias lead us? Low self-esteem or whatever else one may wish to call it is not the real problem. The real problem is sin. Jeremiah 17:9 is true. Because of a deceitful heart, man's tendency is to sustain and enhance his self-esteem. All sorts of positive illusions will be erected and sustained and creative self-deception will reign. As a result the individual becomes vulnerable to extreme theological errors, false doctrines and a false supernaturalism. Dr. David Myers says in his book *The Inflated Self*:

> My primary purpose here is to show how the seductive power of illusory thinking leads to belief in paranormal phenomena, whether or not such phenomena exist. By exploiting the ways people form and perpetuate false beliefs, there is almost no limit to the fictions that can be perpetrated upon credulous minds.[1]

A psychology of self-esteem is a false theology of self idolatry that begins with good intentions but ends up corrupting the faith.

It is often necessary for a transition to occur before an individual will move from one theology to another one that is alien. As personal illusions are established, reinforced and increased, and as self-esteem is encouraged, enhanced and sustained, the individual becomes more open to alien doctrines and even occult activities.

A good example of this transition idea can be seen in the work of Abraham Maslow. Though Maslow is regarded as a key promoter of humanistic psychology, he believed that it was merely a stepping stone to transpersonal or spiritual psychologies. He predicted a move from centering in self to centering in the cosmos, from self-transformation to spiritual transformation. He says:

> I consider Humanistic, Third Force Psychology to be transitional. A preparation for a *still higher* Fourth Psychology, transpersonal, transhuman, centered in the cosmos rather than in human needs and interests, going beyond humanness, identity, self-actualization and the like.[2] (Emphasis his.)

History has proven Maslow correct. Tony Sutich, who founded the *Journal of Humanistic Psychology* was also involved in the beginnings of the *Journal of Transpersonal Psychology*. If one examines the publication of the humanistic psychologists, he will see much that is transpersonal. In her article "A New Age Reflection in the Magic Mirror of Science," Dr. Maureen O'Hara says:

> It is significant to remember that the present New Age movement has its origins in the counterculture of the sixties and early seventies. Early inspiration came from the writings of Abraham Maslow, Eric Fromm, Rollo May, Carl Rogers, and others.[3]

In like manner, history will demonstrate that the self-esteem teachings are merely "transitional," on the

way to false doctrines and false teachings leading to a false Christianity and false supernaturalism.

Charles Huttar has said something to which we add one word: "If man is no longer permitted to have [**true**] faith, he will embrace superstition."[4] It is reported that Archbishop William Temple said something to this affect: "When people cease to believe in God, they do not believe in nothing, they believe in anything."[5] We would add to that and say: When people cease to believe in God or deviate from Him, they do not believe in nothing, they believe in and embrace anything. George Tyrrel puts it this way: "If [man's] craving for the mysterious, the wonderful, the supernatural, be not fed on true religion, it will feed itself on the garbage of any superstition that is offered to it."[6] Christopher Lasch, in his book *The Culture of Narcissism*, tells how the "narcissistic personality of our time, liberated from the superstitions of the past, embraces new cults."[7] When we give up truth we will receive error in its place.

A rise of religious revivalism, the wedding of science and religion, and an increasing fascination with the paranormal all mark our current age. John Naisbitt, coauthor of the best-selling books *Megatrends and Re-inventing the Corporation*, predicts a rising religious revivalism in his book titled *Megatrends 2000*. Those who have studied America can see that a religious revivalism is occurring, especially in the New Age religions. Along with this rise of New Age religions is the blurring of the line between science and religion. Dr. Stanislav Grof, a psychiatrist, says approvingly that "the most advanced developments in science are returning to this ancient knowledge that came from the mystical traditions."[8] The popularity of the paranormal is illustrated by the sales of the Time-Life series titled *Mysteries of the Unknown*. In its first two years the 25-volume series became a best seller. The first volume, *Mystic Places*, sold 1.4 million copies.

The heart of the most prevalent religious revival is humanistic and transpersonal psychology. In humanistic psychology self is god and the therapist is the priest. Transpersonal psychology embraces Eastern religions and all of the religions of the New Age. Unfortunately those Christians whose theologies include psychology and self-esteem are fanning the flames of this false religious revivalism. Moreover they are bringing this revivalism right into the churches.

The wide gate of psychology, with its false facade of respectability, science, medicine, compassion, and tenderness, has already enticed many Christians. Under the guise of so-called Christian psychology, the teachings of Sigmund Freud, Carl Jung, Carl Rogers, Abraham Maslow, Eric Fromm, Alfred Adler, Albert Ellis, and other non-Christians have corrupted the faith of many Christians. Besides that, they have unwittingly prepared many unwary professing Christians to accept New Age heretical thought. Because they think behavioral psychology is science, many Christians do not see that its major theories (of why people are the way they are and how they can change) are simply faith systems which support and feed right into the New Age mentality.

The psychological gates have been erected with the wood, hay, and stubble of the opinions of men. Beneath a veneer of pious platitudes they hide their true foundations of evolutionism, determinism, agnosticism, atheism, secular humanism, transcendentalism, pseudoscientism, pragmatism, paganism, and other anti-Christian "isms." The wide gates include the psychoanalytic, behavioristic, humanistic, and transpersonal psychologies mixed and blended with whatever religious beliefs and practices may appeal to an individual. The catalog of choices is ever expanding, and psychological evangelists hawk many other gospels.

These psychological gates are not only in the world. They are blatantly standing in the church and offering numerous combinations of theories and therapies. They are readily accessible to Christians, especially when they are whitewashed with Bible verses and given top billing in Christian bookstores and on Christian media. Rather than guiding people to the strait gate and along the narrow way, too many Christian pastors, leaders, and professors are pointing to the wide gate made up of over 450 different psychological systems combined in thousands of ways. Rather than calling people to come out of the world and to be separate, they have brought these worldly psychologies right into the church. Rather than open altars, there are wide gates. Indeed, it's almost impossible to avoid the wide gate and the broad way—especially when disguised as the strait gate and the narrow way.

Here is an example from one of Dobson's broadcasts to illustrate how easy it is to slip into the New Age. On the broadcast, a tape is played of excerpts from talks by Norman Cousins. The broadcast includes this disclaimer: "We're not endorsing all his views." However, it would be difficult to know what exactly was endorsed and what was not. Cousins is well-known as a New Ager and a phone number is given for obtaining cassette tapes of his various talks. If a person calls that number he receives a catalog listing a number of other New Age speakers and topics as well.

Cousins is a nonscientist preaching nonscience. On the tape which was aired on Dobson's program, Cousins' theme is the relationship between thoughts and illness. Throughout the tape he develops the idea that thoughts affect physical health. He confidently asserts:

> We do have a large measure of capability for integrating our minds and our bodies and putting both to work in developing our potentiality. Not just in health but in illness.[9]

This is a strong theme in much of the human potential movement and holistic health. We are acquainted with the emerging field of psychoneuroimmunology, which studies the relationship of the human response to experience, the central nervous system, and the body's defense system against disease. Unlike Cousins' assertions, reports on research in this field are filled with the word *may*. For example, one might say that thoughts *may* be related to illness. However, we know of no researcher in the field who would assert that wrong thinking makes you sick. The *Journal of the American Medical Association* reports:

> No significant risk for cancer morbidity or mortality was associated with depressive symptoms with or without adjustment for age, sex, marital status, smoking, family history of cancer, hypertension, and serum cholesterol level. . . . These results call into question the causal connection between depressive symptoms and cancer morbidity and mortality.[10]

Dr. Bernard Fox, a researcher in the area of the mind-body relationship, refers to "the unsettled and uncertain state of this field." He says, "The findings from the literature have been so varied, so mixed, even contradictory in many cases, that **to take a strong position in this field is scientifically dangerous.**"[11] (Emphasis added.)

The University of California *Berkeley Wellness Letter* discusses the mind-body connection in an article titled "Will 'Right Thinking' Keep You Well?" The article concludes by saying, "The connections between the mind and cancer remain unresolved."[12]

On the tape aired on Dobson's Focus on the Family broadcast, Cousins tells a story about a man who lay down on a bed of sharp nails that penetrated his back, apparently without pain. When the man got up his back was punctured with holes but only one site was bleeding. When this was called to the man's attention, he "turned it off" (the bleeding). Cousins says that the man was able to control pain, bleeding and infection. He said that the man trained himself to do this with his thoughts.

Cousins' story of mind over matter with thinking controlling pain and bleeding was at the core of the message Dobson liked. It was obvious that Dobson liked the message since that 20 minutes of speaking had been selected out of four hours of Cousins' tapes. Is controlling bleeding, pain, and infection through thinking a natural process that anyone can and, therefore, should learn? If so, where is the research documentation of double-blind studies done on significantly large numbers of people? After years of this kind of belief, at least since the New Thought of the nineteenth century, some research should have come forth. Or, could this actually be an occultic process?

Why was Dobson attracted to this questionable example from Cousins' four hours of tapes? The Focus on the Family announcer introduced this tape with these words:

> We are fully aware that Norman Cousins does not come from an evangelical Christian perspective, but all truth is God's truth. If it's true, it came from God, and the next twenty minutes we feel are true and valuable and will make a contribution in your life.[13]

Is Cousins' example of controlling bleeding, pain, and infection through some mental process God's truth, man's fantasy, or Satan's lie? Evidently Dobson thinks it's "God's truth," in the same way he believes that his teachings about self-esteem are "God's truth." Faith in psychology and self-esteem certainly softens the soil for suspicious seeds.

In spite of the cry "All truth is God's truth!" psychological self-esteemers are drastically deviating from the truth of God by offering a view of man that contradicts the Scripture. As a result, false commitments to Christ are made based upon a false view of man. And those who know Christ are being weakened in their walk. The self-esteem view of man is a perversion of the biblical view and can only result in false conversions and compromised Christianity.

Self-esteem, secular humanism, and humanistic psychology are all part of what we call the self-syndrome. According to the dictionary a syndrome is "a number of symptoms occurring together and characterizing a specific disease or condition."[14] We would say that the self-syndrome represents a number of symptoms which characterize a "disease" of self. Selfism is an expression of this "disease," selfology is the study of this "disease," and selfolatry is the "disease."

We see selfism and false supernaturalism in ancient Babylon. Isaiah 47:10 reveals:

> For thou hast trusted in thy wickedness: thou has said, None seeth me. Thy wisdom and thy knowledge, it hath perverted thee; and thou hast said in thine heart, I am, and none else beside me.

It was "wisdom" and "knowledge" that perverted the Babylonians until they said, "I am, and none else beside me." The perversion of worldly wisdom and knowledge caused the Babylonians to say, "I am and none else beside me" (Isaiah 45:6). That is equivalent to saying, "I am God."

Isaiah says in Isaiah 47:13:

> Thou art wearied in the multitude of thy counsels. Let now the astrologers, the stargazers, and monthly prognosticators, stand up, and save thee.

In ancient Babylon we see selfism, self-etc., "I am and none else beside me," which led to a false supernaturalism and interest in the occult. The selfologists are paving the way and smoothing the path. The selfologists are helping the move from selfism (a centering on self) to mysticism (a loss of self). From self as the center of the universe to self as a part of the universe. We have moved from a nation of God worshipers to self-worshipers and selfism has been a key element in the change. We say in our book *The End of "Christian Psychology"*:

> Many have run from religion until the emptiness finally caught up with them. Now, instead of returning to the one true God of the universe, they are following the false gods of men's minds. Instead of looking to God, their Creator, many are looking to man as the creator of gods and end up replacing one vacuum with another. Dr. Abraham Maslow is an example of this trend.[15]

The "isms" and "ologies" of self will cause people to take their eyes off Jesus. And no matter what euphemism one may give it and no matter how one may try to justify it, it is a cult of self-worship. The "isms" and "ologies" of self will lead to self as the great "I am" and then into destruction.

The great temptation in the Garden of Eden was when Satan said, "Ye shall be as gods." This was the crux of Satan's fall. Isaiah quotes him as saying, "I will be as the most high" (Isaiah 14:14). Selfism is as old as the Garden of Eden and proclaims the same message. As a nation we have reaped the blessings of God and we have turned to self as a result. The Lord says in Hosea, "as they were increased, so they sinned against me" (Hosea 4:7). In Jeremiah the Lord says, "When I had fed them to the full, they then committed adultery" (Jeremiah 5:7).

Jesus warned, "Be not deceived." The way to heed that warning is to know the Bible and use it critically to evaluate every idea about man with careful scrutiny. Many psychological ideas sound plausible and even attractive. In fact, it is very easy to embrace a particular psychological frame of mind and then to see everything from that perspective. However, Christians are to have a biblical frame of mind. Paul admonished believers:

> Beware lest any man spoil you through philosophy and vain deceit, after the tradition of men, after the rudiments of the world, and not after Christ. For in him dwelleth all the fulness of the Godhead bodily (Colossians 2:8-9).

Paul further declared:

> For the weapons of our warfare are not carnal, but mighty through God to the pulling down of strong holds; casting down imaginations, and every high thing that exalteth itself against the knowledge of God, and bring-

ing into captivity every thought to the obedience of Christ
(2 Corinthians 4-5).

While the world may look for a Utopia conceived in the
minds of men and established with human goodness, Christians are admonished to look forward to the return of our Lord
Jesus Christ. While those who have no hope are busy fabri-
cating a hope that will vanish with the wind, true Christians
have a hope that will not fade away. Let us therefore cling to
the faith once delivered to the saints and keep ourselves away
from the enticements of the psychoheretical gates that lead to
destruction.

14

The Hope
of
Glory

When the Israelites attempted to blend faith in God and trust in idols, God was displeased and allowed disaster to overtake them. He did this for one purpose: to cause them to return to Him. Hear His concern for those who turn to other sources of help:

> Hath a nation changed their gods, which are yet no gods? but my people have changed their glory for that which doth not profit. Be astonished, O ye heavens, at this, and be horribly afraid, be ye very desolate, saith the LORD. For my people have committed two evils; they have forsaken me the fountain of living waters, and hewed out cisterns, broken cisterns, that can hold no water (Jeremiah 2:11-13).

The Israelites continued to be religious and even to follow certain ceremonial rites. But their hope for help was divided. Rather than waiting on God in faith and obedience, they turned to outside methods of help. They incorporated the notions and methods of the heathen nations in hopes of success. They, too, tried to use the "best from both worlds." But, when they did so, they eventually found that God withdrew His hand of help and mercy.

God always desires to show mercy. But, if people trust in idols or in man, rather than in God, they place themselves outside of God's grace.

> Thus saith the LORD, Cursed be the man that trusteth in man, and maketh flesh his arm, and whose heart departeth from the LORD. . . (Jeremiah 17:5).

Yet, if they turn to God and trust Him, they are blessed:

> Blessed is the man that trusteth in the LORD, and whose hope the LORD is. For he shall be as a tree planted by the waters, and that spreadeth out her roots by the river, and shall not see when heat cometh, but her leaf shall be green; and shall not be careful in the year of drought, neither shall cease from yielding fruit. The heart is deceitful above all things, and desperately wicked: who can know it? I the LORD search the heart, I try the reins, even to give every man according to his ways, and according to the fruit of his doings (Jeremiah 17:7-10).

No psychological system can know the heart of man, no matter how many theories and therapies are devised. Only God knows the heart, and God is a rewarder of those who trust in Him (Hebrews 4:12-13 and 11:6).

Dobson and others attempt to offer hope through adding psychological systems, theories, and techniques to the revealed Word of God. But, what kind of hope do psychological systems of analyzing and helping people really have to offer? Paul describes people without Christ as "having no hope" (Ephesians 2:12). Therefore, according to the written revelation of God, Freud, Adler, Jung, Maslow, Rogers, and other secular psychologists were without true hope.

The hope of the Gospel, the hope that thrives under duress, the hope that has held saints steady through the centuries is the hope that is found only in Jesus. It is not an external, psychological hope. It is a living, spiritual hope which comes through relationship with Christ. The glorious truth is encapsulated in one short phrase: **"Christ in you, the hope of glory"** (Colossians 1:27). For that hope Paul was willing to be beaten, left for dead, imprisoned, and finally martyred.

Hope in Christ is not only hope for future glory in heaven. It is hope for His present work in a Christian's life as that believer looks to Jesus for life and change.

> But we all, with open face beholding as in a glass the glory of the Lord, are changed into the same image from glory to glory, even as by the Spirit of the Lord (2 Corinthians 3:18).

Jesus promises:

> If any man thirst, let him come unto me, and drink. He that believeth on me, as the Scripture hath said, out of his belly shall flow rivers of living water (John 7:37-38).

Jesus is faithful to His promise. He sent the Holy Spirit to enable His people to live the new life that He purchased for them on the cross. Therefore, believers have all they need for life and godliness, right attitudes and actions in the sight of God.

God's Word is His revelation to mankind about Himself and about the nature of humanity, how people are to live, and how they change. Furthermore, Jesus died to give brand new life to those who are born again through faith in Him. And the Holy Spirit enables believers to live according to God's Word.

Jesus did not call people to an external system of ethics, but to a relationship that affects every aspect of a person's life and operates every moment of the day or night. Nor did Jesus call people to live in and for themselves, but rather in and for Him and with other believers. Therefore, He compared His relationship to believers with a vine and its branches (John 15)

and with a shepherd and his sheep (John 10). It is a relationship of profound love and intimacy. It is the oneness Jesus
expressed in His high priestly prayer in John 17, when he
prayed:

> Neither pray I for these alone, but for them also which
> shall believe on me through their word; That they all may
> be one; as thou, Father, art in me, and I in thee, that they
> also may be one in us: that the world may believe that
> thou hast sent me . . . that the love wherewith thou has
> loved me may be in them, and I in them (John 17:20-21,
> 26).

What offering of psychology can compare with this opulent
treasure of relationship with the Father and the Son. Even a
brief moment of awareness of this awesome truth is far more
glorious than all of the self-esteem, self-confidence, self-love,
self-worth wherewith one might fill himself.

Those who have been devastated by disappointment, who
have suffered pain inflicted by sinful humanity, and who seek
an end to suffering even unto death will find balm for their
souls in Jesus. Why give them a boost in self-esteem or psychological theories and therapies? Those who have been in
bondage to sin can only be set free through Jesus. All other
methods of overcoming sin are superficial and temporary. Why
mix and blend the systems of the world with the promises in
the Word? Such freedom does not come from a hocus-pocus
kind of faith in faith, but rather through being born again so
that Jesus resides in the believer. Those indwelt by Jesus can
walk by His life and His Word rather than by the old ways.

May the Lord have mercy on those who have exchanged
their birthright for a mess of psychological pottage. May the
Lord have mercy on those who have offered that stew to men,
women, and children for whom Christ died. May the Lord have
mercy on us all and revive His church with a fresh hunger for
His Word, with a renewed confidence in His provisions and
promises found in that Word, and with such love for God and

one another that oneness in Christ (rather than self-esteem) will be our passion and our very life.

As believers pray for cleansing, seek God's face with diligence, put off the old (all that is of the world, the flesh, and the devil) and put on the new (all that is in Christ Jesus), they will find Him faithful. "Let us therefore come boldly unto the throne of grace, that we may obtain mercy, and find grace to help in time of need" (Hebrews 4:16). He gives the true manna from heaven which is Himself, rather than the wisdom of men. He offers springs of living water instead of the broken cisterns of psychological systems. Believers have a glorious hope, not in self, but in Jesus Christ!

Notes

Chapter 1: Reasons for Concern
1. Tim Stafford, "His Father's Son." *Christianity Today*, April 22, 1988, p. 22.
2. James Dobson. *The Strong-Willed Child*. Wheaton, IL: Tyndale House Publishers, Inc., 1984, p. 234.
3. Letter on file.
4. J. Vernon McGee, "Psycho-Religion—The New Pied Piper." *Thru the Bible Radio Newsletter*, November 1986.
5. John Leo, "Damn, I'm Good," *US News & World Report*, May 18, 1998.
6. Robyn M. Dawes. House of Cards: Psychology and Psychotherapy Built on Myth. New York: Free Press/Macmillan, Inc., 1994, p. 58.

Chapter 2: Psychological Savior
1. Michael J. Gerson, "A Righteous Indignation." U.S. News & World Report, May 4 1998, p. 22.
2. Letter from Board of Medical Quality Assurance Psychology Examining Committee, State of California, on file.
3. Tim Stafford, "His Father's Son." *Christianity Today*, April 22, 1988, p. 16.
4. *Ibid.*, p. 22.
5. E. Brooks Holifield. *A History of Pastoral Care in America: From Salvation to Self-Realization.* Nashville: Abingdon Press, 1983, pp. 231ff.
6. Stafford, *op. cit.*, p. 20.
7. Martin Gross. *The Psychological Society.* New York: Random House, 1978.
8. James Dobson. *Dare to Discipline*. Wheaton, IL: Tyndale House Publishers, Inc., 1970.
9. James Dobson. *The Strong-Willed Child*. Wheaton, IL: Tyndale House Publishers, Inc., 1984, p. 40.
10. *Ibid.*, p. 45.
11. *Ibid.*, p. 63.
12. James Dobson. *Hide or Seek*, Revised Edition. Old Tappan, NJ: Fleming H. Revell Company, 1979, pp. 17-20.
13. Dobson, *The Strong-Willed Child, op. cit.*, p. 88.
14. Dobson, *Hide or Seek, op. cit.*, p. 54.
15. *Ibid.*, p. 32.
16. *Ibid.*, p. 59.
17. *Ibid.*, p. 66.
18. *Ibid.*
19. *Ibid.*, p. 60.
20. Dobson, *The Strong-Willed Child, op. cit.*, pp. 50, 52, 55.
21. Dobson, *Dare to Discipline, op. cit.*, p. 10.
22. *Ibid.*, p. 11.
23. *Ibid.*, p. 14.

Chapter 3: Dr. Dobson's Commitment to Psychology
1. James Dobson. *Dare to Discipline*. Wheaton, IL: Tyndale House Publishers, Inc., 1970, p. 157.

2. *Ibid.*, p. 49.
3. *Ibid.*
4. *Ibid.*, p. 25; James Dobson. *Hide or Seek*, Revised Edition. Old Tappan, NJ: Fleming H. Revell Company, 1979, p. 66; James Dobson. *What Wives Wish Their Husbands Knew about Women.* Wheaton, IL: Tyndale House Publishers, Inc., 1975, p. 63.
5. Dobson. *Hide or Seek, op. cit.*, pp. 60, 92-93.
6. *Ibid.*, p. 63.
7. *Ibid.*, p. 146.
8. James Dobson. *Dr. Dobson Answers Your Questions.* Wheaton, IL: Tyndale House Publishers, Inc., 1982, 1989, p. 497.
9. *Ibid.*, p. 498.
10. *Ibid.*
11. Dobson. *Hide or Seek, op. cit.*, p. 17.
12. *Ibid.*
13. *Ibid.*, p. 18.
14. *Ibid.*, pp. 18-19.
15. *Ibid.*, p. 19.
16. *Ibid.*
17. *Ibid.*
18. *Ibid.*, p. 156.
19. Dobson. *What Wives Wish. . .*, *op. cit.*, p. 125.
20. James Dobson, *Emotions: Can You Trust Them?* Ventura, CA: Regal Books, 1980, p. 93.
21. Carol Tavris. *Anger: The Misunderstood Emotion.* New York: Simon and Schuster, 1982, p. 38.
22. Dobson. *What Wives Wish. . .*, *op. cit.*, p. 78.
23. *Ibid.*, p. 82.
24. *Ibid.*
25. *Ibid.*, p. 83.
26. Dobson, *Dare to Discipline, op. cit.*, p. 4.
27. *Ibid.*, p. 49.
28. *Ibid.*, p. vii.
29. *Ibid.*, p. 50.
30. Calvin S. Hall and Gardner Lindzey. *Theories of Personality.* New York: John Wiley & Sons, Inc., 1957, p. 234. Also see, pp. 420-421.
31. Dobson, *Dare to Discipline, op. cit.*, p. 51.
32. *Ibid.*, p. 63.
33. Jay E. Adams. *The Big Umbrella.* Grand Rapids, MI: Baker Book House, 1972, p. 131.
34. Jay E. Adams. *The Christian Counselor's Manual.* Grand Rapids, MI: Baker Book House, 1973, p. 82.
35. James Dobson. *The Strong-Willed Child.* Wheaton, IL: Tyndale House Publishers, Inc., 1984, p. 232.
36. *Ibid.*
37. *Ibid.*
38. *Ibid.*, p. 233.
39. *Ibid.*
40. *Ibid.*
41. *Ibid.*
42. *Ibid.* p. 234.

43. *Ibid.* p. 235.

Chapter 4: Self-Etc.
1. James Dobson. *Dare to Discipline*. Wheaton, IL: Tyndale House Publishers, Inc., 1970, p. 19.
2. .James Dobson. *Hide or Seek*, Revised Edition. Old Tappan, NJ: Fleming H. Revell Company, 1979, pp. 58-59.
3. James Dobson. *What Wives Wish Their Husbands Knew about Women.* Wheaton, IL: Tyndale House Publishers, Inc., 1975, p. 14.
4. *Ibid.* p. 24.
5. Dobson, *Hide or Seek, op. cit.*, p. 21.
6. *Ibid.*, p. 160.
7. *Ibid.*, p. 165.
8. *Ibid.*
9. *Ibid.*, p. 166.
10. Thomas a Kempis. *The Imitation of Christ*. Westwood, NJ: The Christian Library, 1984, Chapter VIII.
11. Stephen Charnock. *The Works of Stephen Charnock*, Vol. III, *The New Birth*. Edinburgh: The Banner of Truth Trust, 1986, p. 21.
12. Stephen Charnock quoted by Arthur W. Pink. *Practical Christianity.* Grand Rapids, MI: Baker Book House, 1974, p. 42.
13. Richard Baxter. *Saints' Everlasting Rest*. Welwyn, England: Evangelical Press, 1978, p. 315.
14. Charles Spurgeon. *Spurgeon's Expository Encyclopedia*, Vol. I. Grand Rapids, MI: Baker Book House, 1985, p. 458.
15. Jim Owen. *Christian Psychology's War on God's Word*. Santa Barbara, CA: EastGate Publishers, 1993, p. 27.
16. James Dobson. *Love Must be Tough*, Waco, TX: Word Books Publisher, 1983, p. 124.
17. Charles Swindoll. *Growing Wise in Family Life*, Fullerton, CA: Insight for Living, 1986, pp. 131-148.
18. *Ibid.*, p. 146.
19. *Ibid.*, p. 138.

Chapter 5: Psychologized Needs, Morals, Acceptance, and Forgiveness
1. James Dobson. *What Wives Wish Their Husbands Knew about Women.* Wheaton, IL: Tyndale House Publishers, Inc., 1975. pp. 12-13.
2. *Ibid.*, p. 28.
3. *Ibid.*, p. 63.
4. *Ibid.*, p. 64.
5. *Ibid.*, p. 117.
6. Robert D. Smith, "Book Reviews." *The Journal of Pastoral Practice*, Vol. V, No. 1, 1981, p. 50.
7. Tony Walter. *Need: The New Religion* Downers Grove, IL: InterVarsity Press, 1985, Preface.
8. *Ibid.*, p. 5.
9. *Ibid.*, p. 13.
10. *Ibid.*, p. 161.
11. *Ibid.*, p. 111.
12. Andrew Murray in William Law's *Freedom from a Self-Centered Life/Dying to Self*. Minneapolis: Bethany Fellowship, 1977, p. 79.

13. James Dobson, "Dr. Dobson Answers Your Questions." *Dr. James Dobson's Focus on the Family Bulletin*, March 1990.
14. Erich Fromm. *Man for Himself: An Inquiry into the Psychology of Ethics.* New York: Holt, Rinehart and Winston, 1947, p. 13.
15. Jay Haley. *Strategies of Psychotherapy.* New York: Grune & Stratton, Inc., 1963, pp. 71, 82.
16. Paul Brownback. *The Danger of Self-Love.* Chicago: Moody Press, 1982, p. 66.
17. "Dr. Dobson Answers Your Questions," *Focus on the Family,* October, 1988, p. 5.
18. James Dobson. *Preparing for Adolescence.* New York: Bantam Books, 1980, p. 143.
19. James Dobson, "Dear Friends,"*Focus on the Family,* July 1996.
20. James Dobson. *When God Doesn't Make Sense.* Wheaton: Tyndale House Publishers, Inc., 1993, p. 238.
21. Robert M. Johnson. *A Logic Book,* Second Edition. Belmont, CA: Wadsworth Publishing Company, 1992, p. 258.

Chapter 6: Dr. Dobson's Theme of Self-Esteem

1. James Dobson. *Dare to Discipline.* Wheaton, IL: Tyndale House Publishers, Inc., 1970, p. 19.
2. James Dobson. *Hide or Seek,* Revised Edition. Old Tappan, NJ: Fleming H. Revell Company, 1979, p. 19.
3. Shelley E. Taylor. *Positive Illusions.* New York: Basic Books, Inc., Publishers, 1989, p. 8.
4. *Ibid.,* pp. 9-10.
5. *Ibid.,* pp. 10-11.
6. Dobson, *Hide or Seek, op. cit.,* p. 20.
7. A. W. Pink. *An Exposition of the Sermon on the Mount.* Grand Rapids, MI: Baker Book House, 1950, 1953, p. 424.
8. Dobson, *Hide or Seek, op. cit.,* p. 152.
9. Michael A. Wallach and Lise Wallach *Psychology's Sanction for Selfishness.* San Francisco: W. H. Freeman and Company, 1983, pp. ix-x.
10. Dobson, *Hide or Seek, op. cit.,* p. 57.
11. *Ibid.,* p. 81.
12. *Ibid.,* p. 84.
13. *Ibid.,* pp. 162-164.
14. Letter on file.
15. Dobson, *Hide or Seek, op. cit.,* p. 147.
16. James Dobson. *What Wives Wish Their Husbands Knew about Women.* Wheaton, IL: Tyndale House Publishers, Inc., 1975, p. 60.
17. Robert Smith, "Book Reviews." *Journal of Pastoral Practice,* Vol. V, No. 1, 1981, p. 56.
18. James Dobson. *Preparing for Adolescence.* New York: Bantam Books, 1980. p. 1.
19. *Ibid.,* p. 9.
20. *Ibid.*
21. *Ibid.*
22. *Ibid.,* p. 10.
23. *Ibid.,* p. 12.
24. *Ibid.,* p. 13.

25. *Ibid.*, p. 25.
26. *Ibid.*
27. James Dobson. *The Strong-Willed Child*. Wheaton, IL: Tyndale House Publishers, Inc., 1984, pp. 190-191.
28. *Ibid.*, p. 191.
29. Dobson, *Preparing for Adolescence, op. cit.*, Chapter 6.
30. *Ibid.*, p. 127.
31. *Ibid.*, pp. 130-131.
32. *Ibid.*, p. 131.
33. *Ibid.*, p. 127.
34. David G. Myers. *The Inflated Self*. New York: The Seabury Press, 1981, p. 24.
35. Dobson, *Preparing for Adolescence, op. cit.*, p. 118.
36. *Ibid.*, pp. 36-38.
37. Dobson, *What Wives Wish . . . op. cit.*, p. 12.
38. *Ibid.*, p. 22.
39. *Ibid.*, p. 58.
40. Letter on file.
41. Letter on file.
42. Dobson, *What Wives Wish . . . op. cit.*, p. 155.
43. Letter on file.
44. Smith, *op. cit.*, p. 57.
45. Dobson, *What Wives Wish . . . op. cit.*, p. 153.
46. Smith, *op. cit.*, p. 57.
47. Dobson, *What Wives Wish . . . op. cit.*, p. 25.
48. *Ibid.*
49. *Ibid.*, p. 14.
50. *Ibid.*, p. 15.
51. *Ibid.*, p. 43.
52. Dobson, *Hide or Seek, op. cit.*, p. 143.
53. *Ibid.*
54. *Ibid.*, p. 145.
55. *Ibid.*, p. 160.
56. Dobson, *What Wives Wish . . . op. cit.*, p. 35.

Chapter 7: The California Task Force on Self-Esteem

1. James Dobson. *What Wives Wish Their Husbands Knew about Women*. Wheaton, IL: Tyndale House Publishers, Inc., 1975, p. 24.
2. California Task Force to Promote Self-Esteem and Personal and Social Responsibility. "1987 Annual Report to the Governor and the Legislature," p. v.
3. Andrew M. Mecca, "Chairman's Report." Esteem, Vol. 2, No. 1, February 1988, p. 1.
4. James Dobson. *Hide or Seek*, Revised Edition. Old Tappan, NJ: Fleming H. Revell Company, 1979, p. 21.
5. Toni Grant, June 26, 1989.
6. *Focus on the Family*, March 1990, p. 10.
7. Andrew M. Mecca, Neil J. Smelser, and John Vasconcellos, eds. *The Social Importance of Self-Esteem*. Berkeley: University of California Press, 1989.

8. California Task Force to Promote Self-Esteem and Personal and Social Responsibility. "Second Annual Progress Report," January 1989, p. 7.
9. Neil J. Smelser, "Self-Esteem and Social Problems." *The Social Importance of Self-Esteem, op. cit.*, p. 19.
10. *Ibid.*, p. 15.
11. *Ibid.*, p. 21.
12. David L. Kirk, "Lack of Self-Esteem is Not the Root of All Ills." *Santa Barbara News-Press*, 15 January 1990.
13. *Ibid.*
14. "Vindication Claimed for Self-Esteem Idea." *Santa Barbara New-Press*, 30 September 1989, p. A-18.
15. *Ibid.*
16. Thomas Scheff quoted in "UCSB Professor Gets $6,000 for a Chapter in State Book." *Santa Barbara News-Press*, 8 January 1988, p. B-3.
17. David Shannahoff-Khalsa. *Toward a State of Esteem*. Sacramento: California State Department of Education, 1990, p. 142.
18. Andrew M. Mecca, "Chairperson's Report." *Esteem*, Vol. 3, No. 6, September 1989, p. 1.
19. California Task Force to Promote Self-Esteem, and Personal and Social Responsibility, "Definition." *Esteem*, Vol. 3, No. 1, February 1989.
20. John Vasconcellos and Mitch Saunders, "Humanistic Politics." *Association for Humanistic Psychology Perspective*, July 1985, pp. 12-13.
21. John Vasconcellos, "Preface." *The Social Importance of Self-Esteem, op. cit.*, p. xiv.
22. *Ibid.*, p. xv.
23. *Ibid.*, p. xii.
24. *Ibid.*
25. Reuven P. Bulka, "Religion and Self Esteem—Between Convergence and Divergence." *Psychologists Interested in Religious Issues Newsletter*, American Psychological Association, Vol. 12, No. 4, Winter 1987, p. 3.
26. *Ibid.*, pp. 3, 5.
27. John Rosemond, "'Feel-good' parenting is hurting our children," *The Charlotte Observer*, August 8, 1996.
28. The National Commission on Excellence in Education. *A Nation at Risk*. Washington: U.S. Government Printing Office, 1983.
29. Arthur Powell, Eleanor Farrar and David K. Cohen. *The Shopping Mall High School*. Boston: Houghton Mifflin Company, 1985, p. 62.
30. Charles Krauthammer, "Education: Doing Bad and Feeling Good." *Time*, 5 February 1990, p. 78.
31. Charles Green, "Student 'Skills' Slipping." *Santa Barbara News-Press*, 10 January 1990, p. A-1.
32. *Ibid.*, p. A-4.
33. Lauro Cavazos quoted in "Read This." *Santa Barbara News-Press*, 15 January 1990, p. A-8.
34. Mary Ann Roser, "Students bad in math, science," Santa Barbara News-Press, February 6, 1992, p. A-1.
35. *Ibid.*
36. James Kilpatrick, "A Formula for Improving the Schools." *Santa Barbara News-Press*, 18 January 1990, p. A-15.
37. "Education Notes." *Online with Adult and Continuing Educators*, Vol. 7, No. 6, February 1990, p. 2.

38. Diane Ravitch, "Tot Sociology." *The American Scholar,* Summer 1987, p. 343.
39. *Ibid.,* pp. 343-344.
40. *Ibid.,* p. 349.
41. Letter on file.
42. John Leo, "The Trouble with Self-Esteem," *U.S. & World Report,* 2 April 1990, p. 16.
43. Aaron Stern. Me: *The Narcissistic American.* New York: Ballantine Books, 1979.
44. Christopher Lasch. *The Culture of Narcissism.* New York: W. W. Norton & Company, Inc., 1978, p. 59.
45. Daniel Yankelovich. *New Rules: Searching for Self-Fulfillment in a World Turned Upside Down.* New York: Random House, 1981, p. xx.
46. *Ibid.,* p. xviii.
47. *Ibid.,* jacket cover.
48. Rollo May, "The Problem with Evil." *Politics and Innocence: A Humanistic Debate.* Rollo May et al, eds. Dallas: Saybrook Publishers, 1986, p. 96.
49. Lasch, *The Culture of Narcissism, op. cit.,* p. 54.
50. Charles Krauthammer, "More Self-Love Isn't the Answer." *Houston Chronicle,* 8 May 1989.
51. *Ibid.*
52. *Ibid.*
53. Dr. Allan Bloom. *The Closing of the American Mind: How Higher Education Has Failed Democracy and Impoverished the Souls of Today's Students.* New York: Simon and Schuster, 1987, p. 178.
54. Michael A. Wallach and Lise Wallach. *Psychology's Sanction for Selfishness.* San Francisco: W. H. Freeman and Company, 1983, p. 196.
55. Letter on file.
56. Adrianne Aron, "Maslow's Other Child." *Politics and Innocence.* Rollo May *et al,* eds. Dallas: Saybrook Publishers, 1986, p. 96.
57. Ibid., pp. 96, 107.
58. William Coulson, "Maslow, Too, Was Misunderstood." *La Jolla Program,* Vol. XX., No. 8, April, 1988, p. 2.
59. Robyn M. Dawes, "The Social Usefulness of Self-Esteem: A Skeptical View." *The Harvard Mental Health Letter,* October 1998, p. 5.
60. *Ibid.*

Chapter 8: God and Self-Esteem

1. .James Dobson. *The Strong-Willed Child.* Wheaton, IL: Tyndale House Publishers, Inc., 1984, pp. 84-85.
2. *Ibid.,* p. 85.
3. James Dobson. *What Wives Wish Their Husbands Knew about Women.* Wheaton, IL: Tyndale House Publishers, Inc., 1975, pp. 185-186.
4. James Dobson. *Preparing for Adolescence.* New York: Bantam Books, 1980, p. 137.
5. *Ibid.,* pp. 137,138.
6. *Ibid.,* p. 138.
7. *Ibid.*
8. *Ibid.,* p. 140.
9. *Ibid.,* p. 141.

10. James Dobson. *Hide or Seek*, Revised Edition. Old Tappan, NJ: Fleming H. Revell Company, 1979, p. 95.
11. *Ibid.*
12. *Ibid.*, p. 62.
13. Dobson, *The Strong-Willed Child, op. cit.*, p. 78.
14. *Ibid.*
15. *Ibid.*
16. *Ibid.*, p. 84.
17. W. E. Vine. *The Expanded Vine's Expository Dictionary of New Testament Words.* John R. Kohlenberger III, Ed. Minneapolis: Bethany House Publishers, 1984, p. 1075.
18. Letter on file.
19. Dobson, *The Strong-Willed Child, op. cit.*, p. 234.
20. Dobson, *Hide or Seek, op. cit.*, p. 57.
21. Dobson, *What Wives Wish . . . , op. cit.*, pp. 28, 64.
22. Gordon H. Clark. *The Biblical Doctrine of Man.* Jefferson, MD: The Trinity Foundation, 1984, p. 73.
23. Dobson, *Hide or Seek, op. cit.*, p. 169.
24. *Ibid.*
25. *Ibid.*
26. James Dobson, "Little Ones Belong to Him." *TableTalk*, December 1988, p. 5.
27. Trevor Craigen. *An Exegetical Foundation for a Biblical Approach to Thinking of Oneself.* Doctoral Dissertation for Grace Theological Seminary, Winona Lake, IN, 1984, p. 43.
28. Vine, *op. cit.*, p. 693.
29. Paul Brownback. *The Danger of Self-Love.* Chicago: Moody Press, 1982, pp. 104-105.
30. Charles Spurgeon. *Spurgeon's Expository Encyclopedia*, 1834-1892, Vol. 1. Grand Rapids, MI: Baker Book House, 1985, p. 458.
31. Matthew Henry. *Matthew Henry's Commentary in One Volume.* Grand Rapids, MI: Zondervan Publishing House, 1960, p. 1220.
32. Craigen, *op. cit.*, p. 43.
33. Dobson, *Hide or Seek, op. cit.*, p. 184.
34. *Ibid.*
35. *Ibid.*
36. *Ibid.*, p. 170.
37. Reuven P. Bulka, "Religion and Self-Esteem—Between Convergence and Divergence." *Psychologists Interested in Religious Issues,* American Psychological Association, Volume 12, No. 4, Winter 1987, p. 2.
38. Dobson, *Hide or Seek, op. cit.*, p. 186.
39. *Ibid.*, pp. 186-187.
40. *Politics and Innocence.* Rollo May *et al*, eds. Dallas: Saybrook Publishers, 1986.
41. Dobson, *Hide or Seek, op. cit.*, p. 172.
42. *Ibid.*, pp. 171, 176.

Chapter 9: Loving Self or Denying Self?

1. James Dobson. *Hide or Seek*, Revised Edition. Old Tappan, NJ: Fleming H. Revell Company, 1979, pp. 185-186.

2. Erich Fromm. *Man for Himself: An Inquiry into the Psychology of Ethics.*
    New York: Holt, Rinehart and Winston, 1947, pp. 128-130.
3. *Ibid.*, p. 130.
4. Dobson. *Hide or Seek, op, cit.*, p. 186.
5. *Ibid.*, pp. 185-186.
6. James Dobson and H. Norman Wright, "The Importance of Premarital
    Counseling." Focus on the Family Radio Broadcast, CS 213.
7. W. E. Vine. *The Expanded Vine's Expository Dictionary of New Testa-
    ment Words.* John R. Kohlenberger III, Ed. Minneapolis: Bethany House
    Publishers, 1984, p. 693.
8. Jay E. Adams. *The Biblical View of Self-Esteem, Self-Love, Self-Image.*
    Eugene, OR: Harvest House Publishers, 1986, p. 73.
9. K. P. Yohannan. *Road to Reality.* Altamonte Springs, FL: Creation
    House, 1988, p. 51.
10. Adams, *op, cit.*, p. 106.
11. *Ibid.*, p. 107.
12. James Dobson quoted by Rolf Zettersten. *Dr. Dobson: Turning Hearts
    Toward Home.* Dallas: Word Publishing, 1989, p. 132.
13. Yohannan, *op. cit.*, p. 63.
14. *Ibid.*, p. 64.
15. Robert D. Smith, "Book Reviews." *The Journal of Pastoral Practice*, Vol.
    V, No. 1, 1981, p. 52.
16. "Firm Control May Benefit Kids," *Brain/Mind Bulletin,* September 1989,
    p. 2.
17. Dobson. *Hide or Seek, op, cit.*, p. 166; James Dobson, "Raising Confident
    Kids in an Age of Inferiority." Focus on the Family Radio Broadcast,
    CS214.
18. Richard Baxter. *Saints' Everlasting Rest*, abridged by Benjamin Fawcett.
    Welwyn, England: Evangelical Press, 1978, p. 315.

Chapter 10: Truth or Self-Deception?

1. Nathaniel Branden quoted by Ken Ogden, "Author's Corner." *Esteem*,
    vol. 2, No. 1, February 1988, p. 11.
2. Sue Berkman, "Body Image: Larger then Life?" *Women's Health and Fit-
    ness News*, Vol. 4, No. 8, April 1990, p. 1.
3. James Dobson, "Raising Confident Kids in an Age of Inferiority." Focus
    on the Family Radio Broadcast, CS214.
4. David Myers. *The Inflated Self.* New York: The Seabury Press, 1980, pp.
    20-21.
5. *Ibid.*, p. 24.
6. David G. Myers and Malcolm A. Jeeves. *Psychology Through the Eyes of
    Faith.* San Francisco: Harper & Row, Publishers, 1987, p. 133.
7. *Brain/Mind Bulletin*, May 1990, p. 3.
8. Shelley E. Taylor and Jonathon D. Brown, "Illusion and Well-Being: A
    Social Psychological Perspective on Mental Health." *Psychological Bul-
    letin*, Vol. 103, No. 2, 193-210, 1988, p. 197.
9. *Ibid.*, p. 193.
10. Shelley E. Taylor. *Positive Illusions: Creative Self-Deception and the
    Healthy Mind.* New York: Basic Books, Inc., 1989.
11. Taylor and Brown, *op. cit.*, p. 194.
12. *Ibid.*

13. *Ibid.*
14. *Ibid.*, p. 197.
15. *Ibid.*, p. 196.
16. *Ibid.*
17. *Ibid.*, p. 197.
18. *Ibid.*, p. 204.
19. *Ibid.*, p. 205.
20. James Dobson, "Preparing for Adolescence," Focus on the Family Radio Broadcast, CS185, March 16, 1990.
21. James Dobson. *What Wives Wish Their Husbands Knew about Women.* Wheaton, IL: Tyndale House Publishers, Inc., 1975, p. 36.
22. *Ibid.*, p. 37.
23. *Ibid.*
24. *Ibid.*
25. Taylor, *op. cit.*, pp. 244-245.
26. *Ibid.*, p. 245.
27. James Dobson. *The Strong-Willed Child.* Wheaton, IL: Tyndale House Publishers, Inc., 1984, p. 235.

Chapter 11: "Can You Trust Psychology?"

1. James Dobson and Gary Collins, "Can You Trust Psychology?" Focus on the Family radio, December 5, 1989.
2. James Dobson and Gary Collins, "Can You Trust Psychology?" Focus on the Family radio, December 4, 1989.
3. Martin and Deidre Bobgan. *PsychoHeresy: The Psychological Seduction of Christianity.* Santa Barbara, CA: EastGate Publishers, 1987.
4. Dobson and Collins, 12/4/89, *op, cit.*
5. Martin and Deidre Bobgan. *Prophets of PsychoHeresy I.* Santa Barbara, CA: EastGate Publishers, 1989, p. 4.
6. *Ibid.*, pp. 4-5.
7. Dobson and Collins, 12/4/89, *op, cit.*
8. Martin and Deidre Bobgan. *The End of "Christian Psychology."* Santa Barbara, CA: EastGate Publishers, 1997, pp. 80ff.
9. Joseph Durlak, "Comparative Effectiveness of Paraprofessional and Professional Helpers," *Psychological Bulletin* 86, 1979, pp. 80-92.
10. Daniel Hogan. *The Regulation of Psychotherapists.* Cambridge: Ballinger Publishers, 1979.
11. James Fallows, "The Case Against Credentialism," *The Atlantic Monthly*, December 1985, p. 65.
12. Jerome Frank, "Mental Health in a Fragmented Society: The Shattered Crystal Ball," *American Journal of Orthopsychiatry*, July 1979, p. 406.
13. Hans Eysenck, "The Effectiveness of Psychotherapy: The Specter at the Feast," *The Behavioral and Brain Sciences*, June 1983, p. 290.
14. Dobson and Collins, 12/4/89, *op, cit.*
15. *Ibid.*
16. "Sexual Disorders—Part II, *The Harvard Medical School Mental Health Letter*, Vol. 6, No. 7, January 1990, p. 1.
17. Dobson and Collins, 12/4/89, *op, cit.*
18. *Ibid.*
19. *Ibid.*
20. Bobgan. *Prophets of PsychoHeresy I, op. cit.*, pp. 244ff and 251ff.

21. Dobson and Collins, 12/4/89, *op, cit.*
22. Dobson and Collins, 12/5/89, *op, cit.*
23. *Ibid.*
24. Carol Tavris. *EveryWoman's Emotional Well-Being.* Garden City: Doubleday and Co., Inc., 1986, p. 447.
25. Dobson and Collins, 12/4/89, *op, cit.*
26. P. Sutherland and P. Polstra, "Aspects of Integration." Paper presented at the meeting of the Western Association of Christians for Psychological Studies, Santa Barbara, CA, June 1976.
27. A. W. Tozer. *That Incredible Christian.* Harrisburg, PA: Christian Publications, Inc. 1964, p. 11.
28. Dobson and Collins, 12/5/89, *op, cit.*
29. *Ibid.*
30. Gary Collins. *Can You Trust Psychology?* Downers Grove: Intervarsity Press, 1988, p. 94.
31. Karl Popper, "Scientific Theory and Falsifiability," *Perspectives in Philosophy.* Robert N. Beck, ed. New York: Holt, Rinehart, Winston, 1975, pp. 343, 346.
32. Carol Tavris, "The Freedom to Change," *Prime Time*, October 1980, p. 28.
33. Jerome Frank, "Therapeutic Factors in Psychotherapy," *American Journal of Psychotherapy*, Vol. 25, 1971, p. 356.
34. Lewis Thomas, "Medicine Without Science," *The Atlantic Monthly*, April 1981, p. 40.
35. Collins, *Can You Trust Psychology? op. cit.*, p. 124.
36. Garth Wood. *The Myth of Neurosis: Overcoming the Illness Excuse.* New York: Harper & Row, Publishers, 1983, p. 3.
37. Collins, *Can You Trust Psychology? op. cit.*, p. 90.
38. *Ibid.*, p. 89.
39. *Ibid.*, p. 90.
40. *Ibid.*
41. Dobson and Collins, 12/5/89, *op, cit.*
42. Collins, *Can You Trust Psychology? op. cit.*, p. 72.
43. *Ibid.*, pp. 72, 90, 94.
44. Thomas Szasz. *The Myth of Psychotherapy.* Garden City: Doubleday/Anchor Press, 1978, pp. 182-183.
45. Franklin D. Chu and Sharland Trotter. *The Madness Establishment.* New York: Grossman Publishers, 1974, p. 4.
46. Collins, *Can You Trust Psychology? op. cit.*, p. 130.
47. Robyn Dawes. *House of Cards: Psychology and Psychotherapy Built on Myth.* New York: Free Press/Macmillan, Inc., 1994 p, 58.

Chapter 12: Dr. Dobson Answers His Critics

1. James Dobson. *Hide or Seek*, Revised Edition. Old Tappan, NJ: Fleming H. Revell Company, 1979, p. 166; James Dobson, "Raising Confident Kids in an Age of Inferiority." Focus on the Family Radio Broadcast, CS214.
2. James Dobson, "A Biblical View of Self-Esteem," Focus on the Family Radio Broadcast, CS530, June 7-8, 1990.
3. Rolf Zettersten. *Dr. Dobson: Turning Hearts Toward Home.* Dallas: Word Publishing, 1989, p. 132.

4. James Dobson quoted by Zettersten, *ibid.*, p. 132.
5. Letter on file.
6. Zettersten, *op. cit.*, p. 124.
7. Dobson quoted by Zettersten, *ibid.*, p. 132.
8. *Ibid.*
9. *Ibid.*
10. *Ibid.*, pp. 132-133.
11. *Ibid.*, p. 133.
12. *Ibid.*
13. *Ibid.*
14. *Ibid.*
15. Rodney Skager and Elizabeth Kerst, "Alcohol and Drug Use and Self-Esteem: A Psychological Perspective." *The Social Importance of Self-Esteem.* Andrew M. Mecca, Neil J. Smelser, and John Vasconcellos, eds. Berkeley: University of California Press, 1989, p. 249.
16. Harry H. L. Kitano, "Alcohol and Drug Use and Self-Esteem: A Sociological Perspective." *The Social Importance of Self-Esteem, op. cit.*, pp. 298-299.
17. Jonas Robitscher. *The Powers of Psychiatry.* Boston: Houghton Mifflin Company, 1980, p. 410.
18. Martin Gross. *The Psychological Society.* New York: Random House, 1978, pp. 45-46.
19. Kitano, *op. cit.*, p. 320.
20. *Ibid.*
21. "Firm Control May Benefit Kids." *Brain/Mind Bulletin*, September 1989, p. 2.
22. Susan B. Crokenberg and Barbara A. Soby, "Self-Esteem and Teenage Pregnancy." *The Social Importance of Self-Esteem, op. cit.*, p. 155.
23. *Ibid.*
24. Thomas J. Scheff, Suzanne M. Retzinger, and Michael T. Ryan, "Crime, Violence, and Self-Esteem." *The Social Importance of Self-Esteem, op. cit.*, p. 167.
25. *Ibid.*
26. John D. McCarthy and Dean R. Hoge, "The Dynamics of Self-Esteem and Delinquency." *American Journal of Sociology*, Vol. 90, No. 2, p. 407.
27. Dobson quoted by Zettersten, *op. cit.*, p. 133.
28. *Ibid.*, pp. 133-134.
29. *Ibid.*, p. 134.

Chapter 13: The Primrose Path
1. David Myers. *The Inflated Self.* New York: The Seabury Press, 1980, p. 83.
2. Abraham Maslow. *Toward a Psychology of Being* (1962). Princeton, N.J: D. Van Nostrand Company, Inc., 1968, pp. iii-iv.
3. Maureen O'Hara, "A New Age Reflection in the Magic Mirror of Science." *The Skeptical Inquirer*, Vol. 13, Summer 1989, pp. 368-374.
4. Charles Huttar, "The Outer Space Connection." *Church Herald*, April 30, 1976, pp. 24-25.
5. Myers. *op. cit.*, p. 94.
6. George Tyrrel quoted by Madeleine l'Engle. *A Circle of Quiet.* New York: The Seabury Press, 1972, p. 111.

7. Christopher Lasch. *The Culture of Narcissism*. New York: W.W. Norton & Company, 1979, dust jacket.

8. Stanislav Grof interview, *Sounds True Audio Catalog,* 1989-90, p. 24.

9. Norman Cousins' talk on the relationship between thoughts and illness aired on Focus on the Family.

10. Alan B. Zonderman, Paul T. Costa, Robert R. McCrae, "Depression as a Risk for Cancer Morbidity and Mortality in a Nationally Representative Sample." *Journal of the American Medical Association,* Vol. 262, No. 9, 1 September 1989, p. 1191.

11. Bernard Fox quoted in "Author Interview." *Advances*, Vol. 5, No. 4, p. 57.

12. *Berkeley Wellness Letter*. University of California, September 1988, p. 1.

13. Announcer's remarks preceding the Norman Cousins' tape on the relationship between thoughts and illness aired on Focus on the Family.

14. *Webster's New World Dictionary*. New York: Simon and Schuster, 2nd College Edition, David B. Guralnik, ed., 1970-1984.

15. Martin and Deidre Bobgan. *TThe End of "Christian Psychology"*: Santa Barbara, CA: EastGate Publishers, 1997, p. 120.

OTHER BOOKS FROM EASTGATE

Competent to Minister: The Biblical Care of Souls by Martin and Deidre Bobgan encourages believers to care for one another in the body of Christ and demonstrates that God enables them to do so without incorporating the methods of the world. Contains much practical information for developing personal care ministries within the local fellowship of believers. Topics include overcoming obstacles to caring for souls, salvation and sanctification, caring for souls inside and out, ministering mercy and truth, caring for one another through conversation and practical helps, cautions to heed in caring for souls. This book exposes the professional, psychological intimidation that has discouraged Christians from ministering to one another during trials and temptations. It both encourages and reveals how God equips believers to minister to one another. 262 pages, soft bound, ISBN 0-941717-11-9.

12 Steps to Destruction: Codependency/Recovery Heresies by the Bobgans provides information for Christians about codependency/recovery teachings, Alcoholics Anonymous, Twelve-Step groups, and addiction treatment programs. All are examined from a biblical, historical, and research perspective. The book urges believers to trust the sufficiency of Christ and the Word of God instead of Twelve-Step and codependency/recovery theories and therapies. 256 pages, soft bound, ISBN 0-941717-05-4.

Christian Psychology's War on God's Word: The Victimization of the Believer by Jim Owen is about the sufficiency of Christ and how "Christian" psychology undermines believers' reliance on the Lord. Owen demonstrates how "Christian" psychology pathologizes sin and contradicts biblical doctrines of man. He further shows that "Christian" psychology treats people more as victims needing psychological intervention than sinners needing to repent. Owen beckons believers to turn to the all-sufficient Christ and to trust fully in His ever-present provisions, the power of His indwelling Holy Spirit, and the sure guidance of the inerrant Word of God. 215 pages, soft bound, ISBN 0-941717-08-9.

OTHER BOOKS FROM EASTGATE

The End of "Christian Psychology" by Martin and Deidre Bobgan discusses research about the question,"Does psychotherapy work?" analyzes why Christians use psychological counseling, and gives evidence showing that professional psychotherapy with its underlying psychologies is questionable at best, detrimental at worst, and a spiritual counterfeit at least. The book includes descriptions and analyses of major psychological theorists and reveals that "Christian psychology" involves the same problems and confusions of contradictory theories and techniques as secular psychology. This book presents enough biblical and scientific evidence to shut down both secular and "Christian psychology." 290 pages, soft bound, ISBN 0-941717-12-7.

PsychoHeresy: The Psychological Seduction of Christianity by Martin and Deidre Bobgan exposes the fallacies and failures of psychological counseling theories and therapies for one purpose: to call the Church back to curing souls by means of the Word of God and the work of the Holy Spirit rather than by man-made means and opinions. Besides revealing the anti-Christian biases, internal contradictions, and documented failures of secular psychotherapy, *PsychoHeresy* examines various amalgamations of secular psychologies with Christianity and explodes firmly entrenched myths that undergird those unholy unions. 272 pages, soft bound, ISBN 0-941717-00-3.

Four Temperaments, Astrology & Personality Testing by the Bobgans answers such questions as: Do the four temperaments give valid information? Are there biblically or scientifically established temperament or personality types? Are personality inventories and tests valid ways of finding out about people? How are the four temperaments, astrology, and personality testing connected? Personality types and tests are examined from a biblical, historical, and research basis. 214 pages, soft bound, ISBN 0-941717-07-0.

OTHER BOOKS FROM EASTGATE

Larry Crabb's Gospel by Martin and Deidre Bobgan evaluates Crabb's integration of psychology and Christianity. The book demonstrates that, though he sounds biblical, his teachings are dependent on unscientific psychological opinions. It also reveals Crabb's increasing influence in psychologizing the Christian walk and turning churches into personal growth communities through his mixture of psychology and theology. 210 pages, soft bound, ISBN 0-941717-14-3.

CRI Guilty of Psychoheresy? by Martin and Deidre Bobgan responds to *Christian Research Journal*'s four-part series, "Psychology & the Church" by Bob and Gretchen Passantino. The Bobgans demonstrate that CRI leaves an open door to integrating psychotherapy and its underlying psychologies with the Bible. They present both biblical and research reasons why this open door constitutes psychoheresy, which is a departure from the biblical doctrines of the sufficiency of Christ and of the sanctification of the believer. CRI must now accept part of the responsibility for the church's ongoing capitulation to and use of psychotherapy. 150 pages, soft bound, ISBN 941717-13-5.

Against "Biblical Counseling": For the Bible by Martin and Deidre Bobgan is about the growing biblical counseling movement and urges Christians to return to biblically ordained ministries and mutual care in the Body of Christ. It is an analysis of what biblical counseling is, rather than what it pretends or even hopes to be. Its primary thrust is to call Christians back to the Bible and to biblically ordained ministries and mutual care in the Body of Christ, "For the perfecting of the saints, for the work of the ministry, for the edifying of the body of Christ" (Ephesians 4:12). 200 pages, soft bound, ISBN 0-941717-09-7.

For a sample copy of a free newsletter about the intrusion of psychological counseling theories and therapies into Christianity, please write to:

PsychoHeresy Awareness Ministries
4137 Primavera Road
Santa Barbara, CA 93110

or

phone: 1-800-216-4696

e-mail: bobgan@psychoheresy-aware.org

Web Site Address:
www.psychoheresy-aware.org